EDUCATION
AND
THE AMERICAN DREAM

The Allen-White High School Story 1905-1970

TO: Mrs. Smith:
  Congratulations on your efforts!
You are to be commended on your success.
  "TO God Be The Glory".

Evelyn C. Robertson Jr.

07/22/19

Evelyn C. Robertson Jr.

TABLE OF CONTENTS

FOREWORD

Prior to the advent of integration, a myriad of schools existed solely for the purpose of "training the minds" of African American students. Literally dotting every community's landscape, these educational shrines issued passports to the world for students who dared to dream. These schools were the hub of activity for their respective communities. Many schools held events ranging from "box suppers" to "pie struts" as fundraising efforts in support of the school's operation. A plethora of stories, reports, and testimonies abound supporting the signal impact made by these early institutions.

Prominent among these schools was Allen-White High School, located in Whiteville, Tennessee. Founded in 1905, a mere forty years after the end of the Civil War, this school's growth and development stood squarely on the shoulders of staunch educational trailblazers. This bevy of trailblazers included intellectuals as well as "salt of the earth" tenant farmers who placed the greatest value on education and its benefits.

Education and the American Dream: The Allen-White High School Story, 1905 - 1970 uniquely chronicles and renders with compelling recall this saga in education history. As you read, you will experience Allen-White's trials and triumphs as the school that sired a

legion of educated and resilient people who were dubiously proud to call Allen-White School their home.

While Allen-White's demise came with the 1970 graduating class, the school's impact will no doubt ripple throughout the ages. Author, Evelyn C. Robertson Jr. has produced a high quality addition to the current literature on African American education. As you read, no doubt you, like I will be informed, inspired and perhaps even left chanting an Allen-White team fight song:

Allen-White Bears are on the Floor
Allen-White Bears are ready to go
Allen-White Bears will beat and so
Beware – Beware – Beware

Dr. Jerry Woods

ACKNOWLEDGEMENTS

This book has been simmering in my mind for decades. I am aware of numerous efforts over the years to chronicle the history and legacy of Allen-White School. Bits and pieces of its history have been the subject of several master's theses, newspaper articles, and at least one doctoral dissertation.

My family's roles, dating to the early history of the school with my grandfather, Crawford Robertson, serving as a trustee; my aunt, Myrtle L. Robertson, who taught Home Economics there for forty years; my uncle, Johnny Robertson, who was the first bus driver; my uncle, Vivian Lafayette Robertson, who later served as a trustee; my mother, Pearl Robertson, who served as the cafeteria manager for over twenty-five years; and my aunt, Mattie Brewer, who was a member of the first graduating class in 1933, have all provided me inspiration. I will forever be grateful to Pearl Robertson and Myrtle L. Robertson for their presence is a constant in my life.

Allen-White School provided the foundation that enabled me to compete in a global, multi-cultural society, and any success that I might have amassed I attribute to the administration and faculty. I am grateful to the dedicated and committed teachers and staff.

I would like to thank Dr. Jerry W. Woods for permission to use assorted portions of his dissertation related to Allen-White School, "The Julius Rosenwald Fund School Program: A Saga in the Growth and Development of African American Education in Selected West Tennessee Communities." The personal interviews conducted by Dr. Woods added immensely to my desire to personalize this work. I will be forever grateful to him for his support in this endeavor. I am grateful to Major A. Jarrett for affording me my first professional job in 1962.

I also would like to thank those who encouraged me, and who patiently reflected on my questions and gave me the benefit of their recall. I would especially like to thank Lois Taylor Woods, my friend and classmate, who suggested that I should write this book. I also would like to thank Jeff Sisk, Director of the Tennessee Technology Center at Whiteville, TN, and student Aaron Sims for their computer assistance.

Last but not least, I would like to thank my family for their support and patience over these many months as I have toiled to bring this project to fruition.

I will end by saying that my life has been tremendously enriched through my experiences at Allen-White School, and a huge debt to the pioneers is owed.

INTRODUCTION

Whiteville, Tennessee is situated in the Northwest portion of Hardeman County. The town traces its history to Dr. John White, who moved to Hardeman County from Virginia in the early 1800s and established a trading post in the "wilderness." His Whiteville Trading Post was located at the east end of the modern Whiteville street named Norment Lane. His is one of the earliest known settlements in Hardeman County. Following the signing of a treaty with the Chickasaw Indians in 1818, other settlers began arriving at the Whiteville Post and settled nearby along the banks of Clear Creek. The first stage line passed through the settlement as early as 1821.

By the 1830s, Whiteville had a post office, school, doctors, lawyers, three stores, one hotel, one saloon, and a blacksmith's shop. In 1856, the Jeffersonian Institute was erected. This school emphasized music and art.

My desire to write this book stems from my interest to chronicle, in one location, the efforts of many black citizens in Whiteville to advance the cause of education for their children in the early twentieth century. The early nineteen hundreds was a period in which second-class citizenship for blacks was the norm rather than the exception. The agrarian society of that era found blacks engaged in farming as the principal occupation of that period. During this time, there were few black landowners, as most blacks found themselves working as tenant farmers and sharecroppers. There were few exceptions. Through discussion with my family, I am aware that there was a shoe cobbler and a dry cleaner operated and owned by blacks in Whiteville. The shoe cobbler, Mr. Clay Crowder, sold the land that ultimately became the Allen-White School. Early records indicate the county's first hand-operated merry-go-round inventor and operator, the first jeweler, and the first dry cleaning operator were members of Whiteville's African American community. The dry cleaner was operated by Mr. Fred Tisdale. The community formed its own co-op and soda fountain, had two attorneys, and Dr. Gilbert A. Shelton was a prominent African American physician who practiced in Whiteville.[1]

My intrigue with the efforts and solidarity of the community to provide education and training for its children has been a constant with me for many years. The role that my family played in the education initiative is significant as well.

The social, economic, and political atmosphere throughout Whiteville, Hardeman County, Tennessee, and the South in general was not conducive to supporting education for blacks. Little or no support was provided by the local government, which meant that any efforts engendered required the community leaders, parents, and interested citizens to pool whatever resources they had in order to begin the schooling process. Nationally, there were obstacles in the form of federal laws, which promoted segregation of the races.

There has been much debate among historians over the origins of racial segregation in this country in the decades since emancipation. One group of scholars has argued that segregation was not a predestined pattern of racial relations in the post-war South. Don Boudreaux, Thomas Sowell, Robert Higgs, and Jennifer Roback-Morse offer interesting perspectives in their writings on the history of segregation in this country. White masters and black slaves had lived and worked in close proximity before the Civil War and a variety of patterns of racial relations existed in the 1870s and 1880s. Although southern states did not erect the legal structures that supported an extensive system of social, economic, and political segregation until the 1890s, white hostility had permeated southern race relations for over two centuries. What is certain is that the traditions of racism, white hostility toward blacks, and the inability of the black minority to protect themselves after northern troops went home, disadvantaged the former slaves from the start.

Every southern state had enacted black codes immediately after the war to keep the former slaves under tight control. After these had been voided by the union government, white southerners began exploring other means to maintain their supremacy over blacks. Southern legislature's enacted criminal statutes that invariably prescribed harsher penalties for blacks than for whites convicted of the same crime, and erected a system of peonage that survived into the early twentieth century.

In an 1878 case, the Supreme Court ruled that the states could not prohibit segregation on common carriers, such as railroads, streetcars, or steamboats. Twelve years later, it approved a Mississippi statute requiring segregation on intrastate carriers. In doing so, it acquiesced in the South's solution to race relations.

In the best known of the early segregation cases, Plessy v. Ferguson (1896), Justice Billings Brown asserted that distinctions based on race did not run afoul of either the Thirteenth or Fourteenth Amendments, two of the Civil War amendments passed to abolish slavery and secure the legal rights of former slaves. Although nowhere in the opinion can the phrase "separate but equal" be found, the court's rulings approved legally enforced segregation, as long as the law did not make facilities for blacks inferior to those of whites.

Plessy v. Ferguson served as the basis for legal separation of the races for education until being struck down by the Brown v. Board of Education Supreme Court ruling in 1954. As history has proven, there was nothing equal about the early education of blacks in the early nineteenth century.[2]

The Allen-White Story is not an exception in its formation and development. Interested parents, educators, and citizens in general throughout the South were experiencing the same conditions of deprivation, exclusion, and disenfranchisement. They desired to elevate their children to a level of self sufficiency, and they realized that education was the way to do it. Their sacrifices, selfless efforts, and genuine commitments were demonstrated thousands of times during this era throughout the South. They represent the basis for this writing. Booker T. Washington once said, "At the bottom of education, at the bottom of politics, even at the bottom of religion, there must be for our race economic independence." He also said, "I have learned that success is to be measured not so much by the position that one has reached in life, as by the obstacles which he has overcome while trying to succeed."[3]

1. *Hardeman County Tennessee 2007-2008 Community Guide* (Bolivar, TN: Bolivar Bulletin-Times, year?), 56.
2. C. Vann Woodard, *The Strange Career of Jim Crow,* 2nd ed. (New York: Oxford Press, 1966), 121.
3. Brainy Quote, "Booker T. Washington," http://www.brainyquote.com/quotes/author /b/booker_t_Washington.html (accessed 06/21/08).

CHAPTER 1

Hardeman County Early Education

I would be remiss if I did not discuss the earliest advent of education in Hardeman County, even though the trajectory for blacks and whites took different paths. The first schools for the education of the children of early settlers in Hardeman County were established in 1823. Edwin Crawford and Henry Thompson are credited with being the first school teachers.

In the earliest period, from 1826 to 1873, the "Academy" was the recognized charter school of that day. Prior to 1873, there were six academies chartered by the legislature in Hardeman County—the Bolivar Male Academy, the Bolivar Female Academy, the Lafayette Male and Female Academies, the Enon Academy, the New Castle Female Institute, and the Middleburg Male and Female Academies.

There is no evidence to prove that the Enon Academy and the Middleburg Male and Female Academies were ever in operation. These academies were chartered by the state legislature as corporations—they had boards of trustees and the all rights and statutes of a corporation.

They derived their income from a common school fund received by the county from the state for the sale of public lands, lotteries, and tuition fees. A lottery to raise four thousand dollars to erect a Female Academy was authorized by the legislature in 1826.

The tuition fees for the Bolivar Academies, in 1832, ranged from $7.50 for the first class to $15 for the fourth class. French class was $5, extra drawing and painting classes were $7 to $9, and music was $2.

There is evidence that both the Bolivar Academies and the Lafayette Academy were housed in brick buildings. These six chartered academies and two non-chartered schools were the chief institutions of learning during the early history of Hardeman County.

No definite school program was carried on, and very little is known about their equipment. Mathematical instruments, a sepia, outline maps, drugs, chemicals, and desks were given as articles purchased by the trustees of Bolivar Male Academy.

The teachers were hired on their powers of discipline, as much as on their educational qualifications. The teachers' ability to wield the rod and save the child was an important prerequisite. To be successful, a teacher needed a strong, dynamic personality, which would attract and hold the public, because the school was supported mainly by the tuition fees.

The public school system for the county was established in 1874, and in the period between 1873 and 1891 there was a gradual change from the academies to consolidated schools. This was brought about by an act of legislature in 1873, enabling private schools to acquire public funds by teaching elementary pupils in the district.

The act of the Tennessee Legislature in 1891 caused the decline and eventual death of the academies. Support of the secondary schools by taxation had its beginning in this act, and education up to the eighth grade was supported by county funds.

In 1914, the county court established the county's high schools. Eight were established and were in operation by the 1914/1915 school year. They were on the county unit plan. Bolivar, as the central high school, offered four years of high school work; Whiteville offered three years; and all others offered two years. After 1930, the county established four four-year high schools and five two-year high schools for white children, and two for black children.

In 1850, the earliest date which figures could be found, there were 264 pupils enrolled in the academies in Hardeman County. In 1939, the enrollment of all the public schools, both white and black, was 5,621.

Parents began to pool resources around 1925 and began paying to have their children transported. Wagons were the main mode of transportation. Some of these wagons were similar to the old covered wagons of pioneer days.

In 1935 to 1936, there were eighty-two schools in Hardeman County. These schools were mainly one and two-teacher schools. The schools were near most of the students' homes – walking distance. Those who lived too far from school rode horseback. No public transportation was available.

Later, the state began providing transportation. The board of education contracted with various drivers to furnish transportation with home-made bus bodies built onto trucks or factory built buses. For the year ending 1939, there were five wagons used for transportation, thirty-four regular buses, one automobile, and three pick-up trucks. These transported two thousand students. During this period, there were fifty-one one-teacher schools and fourteen schools with three or more teachers. This was a total of seventy-one schools.

During the early 1940s, the county school board began its own transportation system.[1]

1. Mecoy Ross and Quinnie Armour, "The First Schools of Hardeman County," *Bolivar Bulletin-Times*, July 04, 1976, 3-4.

CHAPTER 2

Earliest Known Education
of Blacks in Hardeman County

The provision for the education of blacks in Hardeman County is traced back to the Civil War. It was then, through the progress of the Union Army in 1862 in the lower Mississippi Valley, that confederate planters deserted their plantations. As a result, the black slaves rushed into the camps of the union forces. General U. S. Grant appointed Chaplain John Eaton Jr. to make provisions for their welfare. Upon Eaton's invitation in 1865, the Western Freedmen's Aid Commission sent teachers among blacks who had been placed in camps at Grand Junction, Tennessee, in the southwestern part of the county. Training programs were started for blacks, consisting of common school training for the youths and industrial and domestic training for the adults. This was the beginning of education for blacks in Hardeman County. The program continued until Eaton was appointed the state superintendent of public schools, according to the Public School Law of 1867, which required that each civil district in the state establish one or more special schools for black children when the official number exceeded twenty-five. This was enacted to afford blacks, as far as practicable, the advantage of a common school education. By 1873, there were 120 blacks between the ages of six and eighteen enrolled in schools in Hardeman County. Ten African Americans had been given limited certificates to teach.

To better prepare the certified teachers, and those aspiring to become teachers, institutes were held during summer vacations and on Saturdays. Teaching certificates were awarded on the basis of state examinations. The most qualified (usually college graduates) or those who passed the examination, served as teachers for the institute. Those persons who passed the examination were assigned schools throughout the county.

The schools were held in churches, vacant houses, and brush arbors. School terms were from three to five months in length. It was common for one teacher to instruct one hundred pupils in grades one through eight. Equipment for the schools included a registry, water bucket, a dipper, a broom, a few erasers, and a box of chalk. No black boards were available, but one wall of the building was painted black.

The Public School Law of 1925 provided for a system of education, to consist of elementary and high schools as well as three state teacher's colleges. It was around this time that the Julius Rosenwald Foundation Program was enacted. The Rosenwald program provided funds on a matching basis for Negro school buildings. Negro citizens purchased the land and the Rosenwald Fund provided the building. Not all communities could qualify for this program, so many of them built schools with their own resources.[1]

1. Mecoy Ross and Quinnie Armour, "The First Schools of Hardeman County," *Bolivar Bulletin-Times*, July 04, 1976, 3-4.

CHAPTER 3

The
Jesse Christopher Allen Dream

H.C.T.S.
ERECTED 1920
TRUSTEES
J.C.ALLEN,FOUNDER ★
WM.MURPHY, CHR.
DR.G.A.SHELTON,SEC'Y.
C.ROBERTSON,TREAS.
ISAM MILLER ★
J.N.NORMENT ★
ED CRISP,SR. ★
J.WILSON, SR.
H.McKINNEY
F.BAIRD
S.W.J.ALLEN
G.FITZHUGH
J.REYNOLDS
WM.MURPHY, JR.
J.H.WHITE, PRIN.

The earliest recorded efforts to educate blacks in Whiteville are attributed to Jesse Christopher Allen. Allen was born August 01, 1864 and died August 19, 1921. His parents were Ephraim Allen and Elizabeth Carnes Allen, who were former slaves in Whiteville, TN.

Mr. Allen manifested an unusual craving to learn, and made rapid progress in public school. He entered Roger Williams University in Nashville, Tennessee at a very young age. There he learned the rudiments of music and tailoring. He graduated in 1884 with honors. After his graduation, he went back to his home community and taught his skills to others in various rural schools for $25 per month.

Mr. Allen met and married Ada Neely, who also graduated from Roger Williams University in 1886 and was a teacher in the Hardeman County Schools.

In 1900, a small school located near Whiteville was moved to a hill in the town; Jesse C. Allen became the principal. The school grew so fast that an annexation was added to the building and a new teacher, Mrs. G. A. Shelton, was hired. The school grew tremendously fast; two more teachers were added—Miss Lena Owens from Memphis, Tennessee and Miss Mattie Tatum Fentress of Chicago, Illinois.

Mr. Allen saw the need to further his education, since the school terms were very short. He was able to do this. He first attended Hampton Institute in Hampton, VA.

By this time, the Rosenwald Foundation, founded by Julius Rosenwald, president of Sears Roebuck & Company of Chicago, Illinois, had come into existence. This foundation provided a sum of money to be matched by the counties wishing assistance to construct adequate buildings for teaching.

At once, Mr. Allen set to qualify Whiteville as a selective site in Hardeman County, and here the perilous and tireless struggles began. The cooperation and assistance of some of the people of the community, with their donations of cash and land, resulted in the completion of the first brick building through the Rosenwald Fund. The school was initially called the Hardeman County Training School. A board of trustees oversaw the funding and completion of the work of the building.

Mr. Allen was a Christian and contributed much to his church and community. From early childhood until his death, he was the clerk at the Elcanaan Baptist Church. He served as superintendent of Sunday school, as Sunday school teacher, and sang bass in the choir. He organized the Baptist Young People Union.

Mr. Allen was believer in organization. He was instrumental in organizing in the Whiteville chapter of the Masonic Lodge, the Knights of Pythias, and an organization known as Woodman.

His knowledge was seasoned with age, and many eagerly sought his advice and guidance, which he gave willingly.

In the 1931/1932 school year, the school that Mr. Allen founded was made into a four-year high school. The name was changed to Allen-White School. It was named for Mr. Allen the founder and J. H. White, the maker.

Although Mr. Allen did not live to enjoy the fruits of his devoted efforts toward education for black people in Hardeman County, he did lay a great foundation for others to build upon.

Mr. Allen was the father of three daughters and one son. His three daughters were all teachers in the Hardeman County School system. They were Mrs. H. G. Norment of Whiteville, Mrs. Velma Seddens of Bolivar, and Mrs. Mabel A. Lake of Hickory Valley.

The life of Mr. Allen will ever shine as a beacon to qualified scholarship in the county and especially in Whiteville.[1]

1. Earnest Rivers, et al., "In Memory of Jesse C. Allen, Founder of Allen-White School," *Bolivar Bulletin-Times*, July 04, 1976, 4.

CHAPTER 4

Mr. Allen's Death and the Search for a New Leader

y 1918, discontent had been building among the leaders of the community regarding the one building and two teachers, Mr. Allen and Mr. Dupree, the other teacher available for students. Between the two of them, the teachers handled approximately two hundred students yearly in the lodge hall. The space was very inadequate for the four months school was in session, which had been the case for fourteen years.

Community members began to look at ways to enhance their children's education, which they so richly deserved. Erecting an adequate school building and securing additional teachers was the answer. Among the things the people did were visit the Tuskegee Institute in Alabama (conferences were held with the educators there and much information gained); consult with Mr. S. L. Smith, the state agent of the Rosenwald Fund; and consult with members of the state and county boards of education.

Community members were able to secure enough information to start work the latter part of 1919 toward erecting the building that formed the nucleus of Allen-White High School. Negroes of the Whiteville community acquired a plot of land about one fourth of a mile from the shopping district of Whiteville and turned it over to the county as the site for the public school—Hardeman County Training School. Mr. Clay Crowder was kind enough to give that plot, on which now stands a monument to him. He lived in the community, a stone's throw from the school.

In erecting and securing the site, Mr. S. L. Smith was influential. He explained to the trustees the Rosenwald system of matching dollar for dollar. The trustees borrowed $4,000 from Whiteville Savings Bank and the Rosenwald Fund matched the amount.

The building was started in the spring of 1920 after the material had been secured from the Rosenwald Fund and the neighbors of the community. Mr. Fields from Nashville was the contractor.

Before the building was finished, the students were allowed to attend school in the new building in the latter part of the school term. This term began the eight and nine months with Mr. J. C. Allen as principal, and his assistants, Sarah Stockall of Nashville; H. G. Norment, the daughter of Mr. Allen; and G. A. Shelton, wife of Dr. Shelton, one of the trustees.

Mr. Allen was called to the great beyond before he had a chance to teach in the lovely new building. The people were at a loss for a principal. Nowhere around them could they find a man who could step into Mr. Allen's place. Mr. Allen had dreamed a dream—a beautiful dream of success for African American education in Hardeman County.

Once again, the Tennessee Board of Education was consulted. Professor L. L. Campbell was accepted as principal for two years. During his principalship, the school suffered for the lack of leadership. Professor Campbell stayed at sword's point with the trustees. He influenced the people not to pay the pledges that they had made, and left the burden of the interest on the original $4,000 on the shoulders of the trustees. At the expiration of his term, he was immediately dismissed by the board.

Professor G. W. Thomas of Chattanooga was elected as the third principal. His efforts reduced the community debt to $500 for the first year, $400 the second year, and not quite as much in the following years. At the expiration of this term, he gave up the principalship.

The progress of the school had been very slow. The people were beginning to believe that they would never find anyone who could take up where Mr. Allen had left off.

Eventhough their doubts were apparent, there were harmonious echoes of excitement in the making.

Perhaps we never make a fine and worthy plan, or dream that is splendid, but the plan or dream comes true somewhere for somebody's benefit, even if it isn't destined to come true for us. So it was in this case. Mr. Allen had dreamed a dream—a beautiful dream of success for Negro education in Hardeman County. Many had tried to break down all belief that it could ever be true or realized. Hence, we come to the fourth principal of Hardeman County Training School, the original name given to the school.[1]

1. J. H. White, *The History of Allen-White School, 1905-1936* (Whiteville, TN: Publisher?, 1936), 2-3.

J. H. White

CHAPTER 5

The James Herbert White Era

1929 FACULTY

Professor James Herbert White of Gallatin, Tennessee applied for the principal position at the Hardeman County Training School. He was elected by the board to take the principalship for the school term 1928/1929.

Because Professor White was younger than his predecessors, it was the common belief of all concerned that he would do more than those that had preceded him.

His term began well, even though there was a very noticeable lack of backing on the part of the community. He gathered information from available sources as to the amount and purposes of the debt owed by the school. With all the information in front of him, he started on the task of eliminating the debt and building a school.

With the aid of the faculty, A. C. White, his wife; H. G. Norment; L. E. Fitzgerald; Professor J. C. Adams; and G. A. Shelton, Professor White launched the first financial drive that the county had ever known. Through a series of entertainments, much soliciting, and contributing, the astounding figure of $1,179 was raised and paid on the debt. The drive closed on Thanksgiving night and the many patrons who crowded the school building were amazed and thankful for such leadership.

After this astonishing success, individuals in every nook and corner of Hardeman County pledged themselves to the support of Professor White. The faculty was assisted by the board of trustees and the P.T.A., which was made up of loyal parents and friends.

The school, at that time, was an accredited high school in the junior branch, and had six teachers. When parents were convinced that Professor White could do things, they became eager and concerned again about building up their school. So, it was in the second year that another faculty member was added, making a total of seven teachers.

Not only the community had eyes on this seemingly dead institution that had suddenly taken on life, but also the board of education, state supervisors, and the superintendent were all watching it struggle for life.

During the second year of progress, the P.T.A. was more active and the trustees were encouraged. The parents and faculty launched another drive. With the support of all concerned, $3,128 was raised. The debt was paid off in full and the notes burned on Thanksgiving night. The rejoicing was great, and Thanksgiving Day began to mean something living and real to the people of Whiteville.

Additions were made to the physical plant in the form of two buildings. One was a vocational building, which was named for Mr. C. R. Howse, the district commissioner of education. The building was located about one hundred yards from Dorris Hall, the first building, which was named for Dr. Dorris, the chairman of the county board of education. It consisted of three rooms, one for science, one for agriculture, and one for the shop. The other building, Ingram Hall, named for Ms. Katherine Ingram, the superintendent of the public schools of Hardeman County, was a dormitory for teachers and the girls who lived to far to go back and forth every day. Electric lights and city water were added so that the school had modern conveniences. During this year, there was a school paper started, known as the *Hardeman County Mirror*, and a band, which was directed by Professor Lockert.

Hardeman County Training School was accredited and made a four-year high school before the school term of 1930/1931 was opened.

During this year, the buildings were completely finished, needed equipment was purchased, books were added to the library, and the school grounds were improved by the addition of shrubbery. The annual rally raised $2,512. During the following year, a bus line was opened and maintained from funds raised in the rally. The bus covered a distance of sixty-four miles a day, running between Grand Junction and Whiteville and carrying about twenty students. Other improvements were made on the campus. Another room was added to the Home Economics Department, and the old shop was converted into a primary room. Another teacher was added and the preparation of teachers improved.

The first class graduated in the spring of 1933. There were thirteen members in the graduating class, ten of whom attended college.

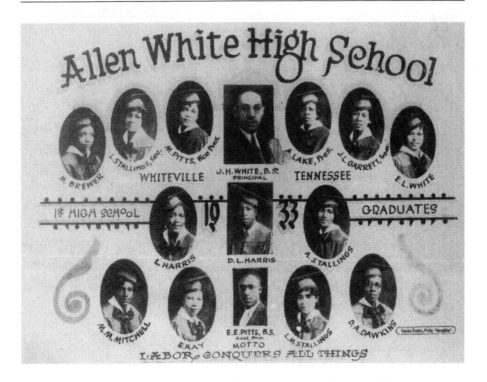

The second class graduated in 1934 with thirteen members, eleven of whom went to college. During this term, there were ten teachers and the school received a "B" rating. The school was represented at the World's Fair in Chicago in the Rosenwald Exhibit in 1932.

The school continued to assemble a strong faculty and grew until it was known in all corners of the state and neighboring states.

A gymnasium, Clift Recreational Hall, a new bus, a sandwich shop, and the principal's home were added to the array of "halls of knowledge" already existing. More volumes were added to the library and scientific and home economics equipment and machines for the shop were added during this period. It was at this time that the institution was on the verge of joining the Southern Association of Colleges and Secondary Schools. The school soon thereafter acquired the second nursery in the state, which made rapid progress under its newly appointed teachers.

The principal, Professor White, served as supervisor of colored schools in Hardeman County for a period of time. He provided to the county teachers his vision of wanting to give black boys and girls a chance to grow into adulthood, fully equipped to meet the world.

The departments at the school were as follows:

The Literary Department

The Literary Department consisted of English and history. The English Department made rapid progress in its strides. It was able to change the worst sort of English spoken into smooth and correct speech. The children were required to master the language. Connected with the department was the Literary Society to which all English students automatically belonged. The instructor was Eddy May Money of Marianna, Arkansas and Spellman College. For their studies, students used the many volumes found in the library on a daily basis.

The History Department

The History Department made great progress. The students who graduated from the institution had an appreciation for the deeds of the great men of the past. Many outside aids or sources were used in the pursuance of the subject—references, current events, National Geographic bulletins, and newspapers. The students selected topics to do research and become more familiar with events directly related to their particular history.Some of the research involved writing to foreign ministers in Washington on their projects. All history students were invited to participate in a history study club, which sponsored all historic movements on the campus. Recitations were held daily in American History, Early and Modern European History, and Elementary Economics. The instructor was Georgia Jenkins of Nashville, Tennessee and A&I State College.

The Vocations

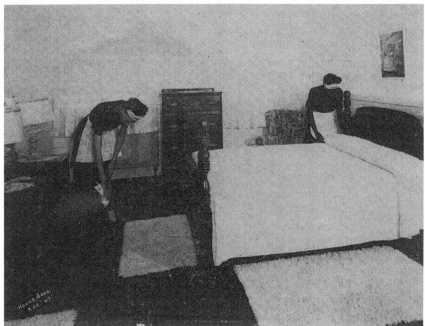

DOMESTIC TRAINING

The Home Economics Department grew rapidly over the years. Instead of one room with a partition made of beaver board separating the Cooking Department from the Sewing Department as earlier, it included nice, large, convenient rooms that were well equipped and attractively arranged. Both sections were inviting to students and they enjoyed their hours of work there. Other than two-year courses required by the state, there was a Maid's Course offered to girls in eleventh and twelfth grade and any other girls who had graduated or dropped out of school. This course prepared the girls for service in the homes of any citizen, no matter how great the responsibilities of society. This program was under the leadership of Myrtle L. Robertson, the instructor from Whiteville, Tennessee and Tennessee A&I State College.

<u>Manual Training</u>

In the Manual Training Department, a dual knowledge of building trades and shop was given. Practical training was given in both. The aim of this course was to prepare boys to enter some phase of the trades after leaving school. In the classes, the boys completed the following types of jobs: Making a U-table for the Home Economics Department; painting

walls and screening buildings; and remodeling the library, a gymnasium, a sandwich shop, and the principal's home. The work was done exclusively by the department. Many cedar chests, lamps, pin trays, ashtrays, tables, chairs, remodeled old furniture, and other such articles and jobs were done by the department as well. The instructor and man to whom the credit must go is William Woods of Selma, Alabama and the Tuskegee Institute.

Cheek Hall is remembered as the centerpiece of the Allen-White Campus. The first Cheek Hall was begun in 1937. Before it was completed, it burned. The second Cheek Hall, began in 1940 with the National Youth Administration (NYA) providing the labor, was completed in 1949. All carpentry work was supervised by Mr. Woods.[1] The Masonry work was done with student labor directed by Dan Green. Mr. Green trained the boys. All brick work and block work was supervised by Mr. Green. All concrete pouring and cement finishing was under the direction of Mr. Roger (Bill) Parham.

A block house was constructed on campus. All four-inch and eight-inch blocks were made in the block house. The bricks were hauled from Bruceton, Tennessee in a truck driven by Worda Sain. The block house

supervisor was Arthur Harris. The boys made the blocks, the block mortar, laid the bricks, finished the cement, and did the carpenter work between classes.[2]

The Agriculture Department

The Agriculture Section provided practical everyday occupations for the students. Each boy had a project. The department repaired the road leading to the school, erected and cleaned privies, kept the lawn trim by working the shrubbery and cutting grass, planted and took care of the school garden, raised pigs and chickens, and helped the farmers understand thoroughly how their crops should be planted and care for. In connection with this department, there was a New Farmers of Tennessee Club, which took part in all farm programs held in the state. The department was under the supervision of Albert Graves of Lucy, Tennessee and A&I State College.

The Science Department

The Science Department included chemistry, biology, general science, and mathematics. The chemistry, biology, and general science classes had sufficient equipment and adequate room in which to work. They engaged in experiments using the chemicals on hand and small animals. There was a terrarium and an aquarium in which animals and plants were kept. Various species of reptiles and other such animals and plants were put in alcohol for class use. Recitations were held daily and laboratory periods were every other day. The instructor was Albert Hardy of Jackson, Tennessee and Lane College. The Mathematics Department was well equipped. There were classes in first and second year algebra, geometry, and trigonometry.

The students appreciated learning how to get mathematical measurements exact without having to measure inch by inch. The subjects were made quite clear and practical by the instructor, Janet Dumas of Nashville, Tennessee and A&I College.

Music

Music was entirely elective. The course consisted of public school music singing. There was a school quartette, a minstrel, and a teacher-trio group (The White Sisters). The quartette, from time to time, won honors at the state symposium and other such contests. The minstrel was very widely known in the state and in adjoining states. It had a cast of boys and girls, chorus girls, and comedians. There was an overture of dances and songs, then jokes, after which was a short play. The group was known to make everyone laugh. The sponsor was A. C. White and Eddye Maye Money.

Athletics

1941 CHAMPIONSHIP GIRLS TEAM
l-r top, Ida Tynes, Helen Shepherd, Emma D. Herron, Martha Woods, Beatrice Woods, Marie Brady, r-bottom Georgia McKinnie, Elizabeth Jones, Addir Bell Williams, Helen Brown

The Allen-White High School (Whiteville) 1938 National Championship basketball team with J.H. White, principal and coach. The picture was made at Tuskegee Institute (now University) in Tuskegee, Ala. where the National High School Basketball Tournament for Colored was held.
Photo courtesy of Alfreeda Lake McKinney

Pictured from left - George Lewis, Mozell Lambert, John Ray, Frank Motley, Jimmie Cross, Walter Lewis, Isaiah Harris & Coach J. H. White, in front

ALLEN-WHITE GIRLS WIN
SECOND IN DISTRICT 27
Players are left to right, front row,
Betty Harris, Barbara Price, Patricia Murphy
Second row, Bernice Newble, Betty Crisp, Dixie
Hunter, Janette Morrow. Third row, Tommie
McKinnie, Bernice Bass, Betty Murphy, Ruby
Bass, Absent Rosemary Jones

Having a keen appreciation of the importance of a sound and healthy body in the maintenance of the highest type of scholarship, the institution encouraged all types of physical exercise and athletic activities. It was the belief of most educators that athletics trained for higher coordination of mind and muscle. To this end, men and women were placed on the faculty who were skilled in various forms of athletics.

The football team demonstrated outstanding skill. They traveled throughout the western section of the state and eastern Arkansas.

The baseball team was noteworthy. The team challenged and held its own in numerous conflicts.

The basketball teams were the pride of the West. Both teams won state championships. The 1940/1941 girl's basketball team won the National Negro Basketball Tournament in Tuskegee, Alabama for two consecutive years. The trophies were proudly placed in the library.

Tumbling was a sport added to the Athletic Department and the girls gravitated to it rapidly.

On the whole, athletics were outstanding among the schools of the state, and the development of the students was an end not too far in the distance, but rather in the grasp of each participant. The coaches in charge were Georgia Jenkins, girls coach, and Albert Hardy, boys coach. Other basketball coaches throughout the school's history included, J. H. White, F. D. Fant, S. F. Fludd, George Meakins, Earnest Rivers, John T. Brady, Alexander Sanders, James Glass, Jesse I. Norment, Evelyn C. Robertson Jr. , and Ernest Wilburn.

The Elementary Department

The Elementary Department consisted of eight grades. The principal was A. C. White, the other teachers were Mamie Smith, H. G. Norment, Janet Dumas, and William Woods. The students pursued the required elementary courses and prepared for the county symposium, which was held in the spring of each year.

The nursery school was included under this head. It was maintained for children who were not of school age. They were treated just as every child should be treated at home—hours for play, rest, and feeding. It was under the supervision of Essie Franklin and Doretha Fitzhugh.

Student Organization

The student organizations available for students were the SUIS Honorary Society, the New Farmers of Tennessee, the Literary Society, the History Club, the Bud Billiken Club, the Culture Club, Football, Basketball, Baseball, Quartette, Chorus, the Laughland Minstrel, and class organizations. The extra-curricula organizations were very instrumental in providing extra training and enhanced self esteem for those students participating.

The Buildings

Upper Left—Ingram Hall (girls dormitory); Upper Right—Howse Vocational Building; Below—Dorris Hall (administration building).

INGRAM HALL, HOWSE VOCATIONAL BUILDING
DORRIS HALL

Allen—White (1) Below—Sandwich Shop; (2) Left—Bus No. 2; (3) Right—Clifft Recreational Hall.

SANDWICH SHOP, BUS NO. 2
CLIFT RECREATIONAL HALL

PRINCIPAL'S HOME

Dorris Hall, the administration building named for the chairman of the board of education, housed the Elementary Department, library, office, Home Economics Department, and the chapel. Howse Vocational Building housed the Science Department, History Department, and shop. It was named for C. R. Howse, the former district commissioner of education. Ingram Hall, the dormitory, was named for Katherine Ingram, the former superintendent of schools. The principal's home, a five room, white frame bungalow was conveniently located near the campus and had modern conveniences, and was cozy and comfortable. The Sandwich Shop was a two room eat shop where boys and girls ate lunch and where patrons visited after school hours for a soda and sandwich. Bus number one was used to transport the children over the sixty-five miles between the most distant home and school. This bus was driven by Johnny Robertson, uncle of the author. Bus number two was used for the minstrel group, teams, and other such organizations. Austin Fentress drove this bus.[3]

Dr. Jerry Woods of Jackson, Tennessee, in his University of Mississippi doctoral dissertation, wrote about Rosenwald schools, which included detailed information about Allen-White High School including personal interviews with former staff and students of Allen-White. In his presentation, he wrote that J. H. White's twenty-year tenure at Allen-White was marked with notable success and unprecedented growth. White garnered both local and national support for the school and its programs. He made numerous valuable contacts as he networked for the cause of Allen-White High School. White was further responsible for visits by several noted civic leaders and philanthropic icons. Among the visitors to the school were noted philanthropist John D. Rockefeller, II and W. I. Meyers of Cornell University. The purpose of their visits was to observe Allen-White's instructional program and to determine if it warranted financial help (White, 1970). Myrtle Robertson described her feelings of meeting John D. Rockefeller, III.[4]

> Believe it or not, one of the Rockefellers, John D. Jr., visited Allen-White School. He came here and people didn't want to believe it. Yes, he came to our school because I spoke to him. It was a special occasion and we had dinner and all of that. Just to look at him was something for us, just to see him. He didn't stay very long, but he came. (Taped interview, February 11, 1995).[5]

Alfreeda Lake McKinney related this description of the typical class day at Allen-White School's Elementary Department:

> Classes began at 8:30 in the morning with devotion. At devotion time we would all come together. We would sing, have scripture, and prayer, and maybe a few words of guidance and inspiration from the principal. We'd sing another song, finish, and then get to work.

> The first thing in the morning was arithmetic because our minds were fresh then. After arithmetic, we had spelling. After spelling, we had health class; that led to the lunch period. In the afternoon, we had science and social studies. There were brief periods in the afternoon for art and music (Taped interview, January 24, 1995).[6]

The school chapel service was also a major part of the school's curriculum. Neola Sardon related her early experiences at chapel as follows:

> When I started the first grade, it was in this little red brick building and all grades one through twelve were housed there. The thing I remember is chapel. My first grade teacher was the pianist. We would have chapel. I knew many of the students from all the grades. Chapel was such a memorable experience (Taped interview, February 20, 1995).[7]

The curriculum also provided opportunities for student expression in the performing arts. Alfreeda McKinney described the closing concert as follows:

The concert was what we called the school's closing play. The closing concert would be near the end of school. Maybe it would be an operetta.

The children would perform. "A visit to Fairyland" was one I remembered.

The play had good fairies and bad fairies. The good fairies wore pink paper dresses. We made the dresses out of crepe paper and the evil fairies wore the green dresses. It was a big event for the community; everybody looked forward to coming to the school closing concert. We had the improvised stage and we used sheets for curtains. We decorated the stage with dogwood blossoms. The dogwood trees would be in bloom in April and we'd attach blooms to the curtain with small nails. It was simply beautiful (Taped interview, January 24, 1995).[8]

The high school curriculum was equally as rigorous as the school's Elementary Program. Allen-White's curriculum met Tennessee's minimum requirement for public high schools—four units in English, one in Mathematics, one in Health Education, three in a major, two each in two minors, and two units in free electives. To implement the instructional program, the principal hired teachers with sound educational training and philosophies congruent with the school's aim. Teachers were recruited from reputable colleges and universities across the country. The teachers who relocated to Whiteville to teach at Allen-White had the opportunity to live in a dormitory located on the school's campus (White, 1979). Bernice Walker Williams, a former Allen-White faculty member, related her experiences of living in the dormitory.

This was my first job right out of college; it was also my first time staying in a dormitory. The single teachers stayed in the girl's dormitory with the young ladies and the married teachers had cottages. I had a roommate who also was a single teacher. We were both music teachers, so we also had something in common to talk about. Professor White's mother was over the dormitory and she took care of the kitchen facilities and all of the people living in the dormitory came together to eat. The teachers ate at a special table. These were the single teachers, men, and women. The dorm was fixed up quite sumptuously (Taped interview, February 20, 1995).[9]

The Home Economics and Industrial Arts programs at Allen-White also were quite productive. The joint efforts of these two departments produced Cheek Hall, which was a prominent building on the school's campus. The girls did the laundry and prepared the meals. The boys made the blocks and completed digging of the basement with a two-handle scoop and a mule. Students also made the beam rafters and performed the masonry work for the project.[10]

Allen-White's curriculum eventually became a model for other schools. The school's academic success impressed Fisk University President Thomas Jones so much that he established an internship at the school under the direction of the Fisk University Education Department (White, 1979).

Perhaps the school's newspaper, *The Allen-White Voice,* _ best expressed the sentiments of the impact of the school and its curriculum:

We feel that our efforts deserve help from the many friends we have throughout America. Our graduates have made good in the fields they have chosen for their life's work and the only advertisement we have is through the boys and girls we turn out (as cited in the Allen-White Reunion Booklet, (September 1994, p.5).[11]

Official comments about the school[12]

"The gateway to success for the colored children of Hardeman County. A monument to the efforts of the colored people of Hardeman County. There is no other institution that serves its purpose better than this school."

(Superintendent W. W. Clift, a graduate of West Tennessee Teachers College, and M.A. from Peabody Teacher's College, superintendent for three years)

"Allen-White High School has been a great success and asset to the colored people of Hardeman County and has played a great part in developing the county in which it is located."

(Dr. Dorris, chairman of the county board of education and medical doctor)

"In addition to being a great influence for good, it is one of the largest assets to our community."

(Mr. C. R. Howse, former district commissioner of education)

"We are fortunate in having Allen-White High School located in Whiteville. They are doing great work among colored people."

(Mayor Prewitt, city mayor of Whiteville)

I am proud that Allen-White High School is in my district. It is the best school for Negroes that I know of."

(R. A. Thomas, former commissioner of education)

Student comments[13]

What Allen-White Has Meant to Me…

"Allen-White High School has really been an asset to me, for it has made me as much a lady as I am today."

"Before I was ever ready to enter Allen-White I had long heard of it. It was known then as Hardeman County Training School."

"I came to Allen-White in the year of 1925 and my teachers were as follows: Mr. H. G. Norment, my home room teacher; Mr. G. W. Thomas, principal; assisted by Mrs. McCulley and Mrs. G. A. Shelton. I was then seven years of age in the second grade."

"At this time, there was only one building on the campus that now bears the name of Dorris Hall."

"When I reached my fourth grade work, I was fortunate enough to enter school under a class teacher by the name of Mrs. J. H. White, and our dear Professor White as principal."

"This year meant more to me than any other I had gone to school, for the leaders were more efficient."

"In the year of 1933, I finished grammar school, at which time I was a member of the 'SUIS' honorary society."

"In the year of 1932, I was promoted to ninth grade at the end of the first semester."

"In 1934, I had finished first year high school work with Allen-White getting bigger and better each year—more teachers, more buildings, more education, and more graduates."

"Under the splendid leadership of Professor J. H. White the school was now an accredited four year high school."

"I spent my second year high school work at Booker T. Washington High School at Memphis, TN, which was regretted very much by me, and in the following year I returned to dear old Allen-White where I started back to work again."

"I was then in junior high school and the school had grown so I was asked to take Maid's Course and Home Economics under the leadership of Miss M. L. Robertson. By this time, I had learned to sew well and was one of the best seamstresses in my class. I won first prize in dress making and accomplished a good many honors."

"In 1936, I began work on my senior year high school. There were thirty-two students in my class, with seventeen being able to finish. My advisor was Miss M. E. Wright, a graduate of Fisk University, Nashville, Tennessee."

"This being my last year, it was the hardest one, for my financial conditions were sparing. Through the aid of Professor J. H. White I was able to secure NYA help, which benefited me greatly the latter part of the year when it was needed most."

"The class of '37 left for the year eight concrete benches, two of them bearing the names of the class officers and members of the class. They are placed in various places on the campus."

"I dare not try to mention all that Allen-White has meant to me, for it has really shaped my career, but now that time has moved on, I am out in the world for myself."

"I'll try and let the Allen-White's motto follow me all the days of my life and live up to it. "Think, Work, and Serve.""

"My teachers have meant more to me than words can express. It would be needless for me to try to write what Allen-White has meant because I feel deep down in my heart something that words cannot explain, and all the credit goes to our dear Professor White."

"May Allen-White have just enough clouds in its life to make a glorious sunset."

Berneece -Student

The impact of the Allen-White School was so formidable that surrounding towns, counties, and states coveted its success. As Minerva Jarrett stated, "They all wanted to be part of Allen-White and the Whiteville Community. Even folks in Bolivar, where the county seat was located." (Taped interview, January 21, 1995)[14]

Former student, Neola Sardon, concurred. She related:

> The school and community were very competitive; people from all over wanted to go to Allen-White. Students would come from many places, as far as Arkansas. My grandmother happened to meet a young lady in downtown Whiteville and the young lady told her the reason she was in Whiteville was to go to Allen-White and that she was looking for a place to stay. So my grandmother said, "I can keep you," so she boarded with my grandmother (Taped interview, February 20, 1995)[15]

A reporter for the Hardeman County Times wrote this of Allen-White's impact on the community:

> Allen-White High School is heard of in all sections of the country for the type of work done through its leader, J. H. White. This school is widely known for its community activities, which sponsor progressive education

in all its phases. The Education Policy Commission rated the school as one of the four leading schools in the United States in carrying out a program of citizenship. The relationship between white people of the county and the school has been good. The school has served a great purpose and in times like these it is fine to have a school like Allen-White (September 06, 1943, p.l)185.[16]

NYA students express appreciation for aid[17]

"I would not have been in school had it not been for the NYA assistance I received. I helped to build the high school shop and now I am able to build small buildings myself. It helped me to learn more about the trade I am interested in." C.V.

"The NYA has meant lots to me. It has helped me to stay in school, buy my paper, books, and some clothing. It has enabled me to learn how to make different things in the shop, such as cedar chests, window frames, and how to lay a foundation to a small building. I hope the work that I have done has given perfect satisfaction." F.M.

"I don't have a father to assist my mother in the home, so I had given up going to school, when Professor White asked me to come back to school and gave me NYA work. I thought it was a dream that I could really go back to school and get some help. I helped to make all the window frames in the Bolivar gymnasium. I worked after school hours in town and I was able to help buy some food to help my mother and go to school also along with learning a trade. I also won the state championship in cattle judging." A.D.B.

"The NYA helped me a great deal. In one respect it has helped me to stay in school. I was out of a job and a far distance from home, with no one to help me. Miss Jenkins put me on the NYA and I returned to school. It also helped me for the practice work that I have done on the campus. I find I take more interest now in doing things because I know better how to do them." J.M.

"As a student of Allen-White High School, the NYA has meant a lot to me. My work began in October as assistant librarian under the direction of Miss Janet Dumas. My daily duty was checking in books and keeping them straight, which I enjoyed very much."

"The amount of money I received was eighteen dollars. With this, I have been able to help my parents who are very old. I have been able to secure my own clothes and school supplies without causing my parents any trouble, and I was very thrilled over my work, which I am particularly interested in." M.Mc.

"The NYA work did not only help me get money to stay in school, but the work I was doing was good practice for me and will help me in my future life work." B.O.

In an article in the *Opportunity Journal of Negro Life*, a group visited classes, talked to the principal, teachers, and students, and watched the boys and girls at work indoors and out. They found that the learning experiences at Allen-White were carefully planned to meet the needs of the homes from which these boys and girls had come and of the lives which they would live when their school days were over. The group found that the students were from no selected group. They were the "run-of-the mine" sons of the African American farmers of Hardeman County and villages of Whiteville. Most of them came from homes of tenant farmers and manual workers. In only one case out of six did their parents own their own homes. Family incomes were barely enough to provide subsistence. Indeed many of the children depended on school for nourishment of body as well as of mind. There were 375 boys and girls, 160 in the high school grades who looked to this school to help them find more abundant living within the narrow limits of tenant farming, manual labor, and domestic service. Back in their homes were fathers and mothers, many of them without benefit of schooling, who had an abiding faith that education could make life better for their children than it had been for them. The Allen-White School was dedicated to an earnest effort to meet these expectations.

"Why have you not added Latin to your curriculum?" A visitor asked Principal White. "The boys and girls of Allen-White have more important lessons to learn," was the reply, "than Caesar built bridges in Gaul. They must first learn how to build bridges, and roads, and fences, and barns, and houses, and sanitary toilets, here in Hardeman County, where lumber stands unused in their fields for lack of man's skill in using it."

The program at Allen-White is simple, but the most important truths are often simple. In the elementary grades, health and the "tool subjects" of reading, writing, and arithmetic are of first concern. This very adequately summarized the commitment of the Allen-White School.[18]

The work of James H. White and his efforts at Allen-White School brought considerable attention from a wider audience. In 1948, White's leadership propelled him from Allen-White High School to the presidency of Lane College in Jackson, Tennessee. White accepted the position at Lane for a two-year period and the college received its first "A" rating under his guidance. After two years at the helm at Lane College, White became president of Mississippi Valley State College in Itta Bena, Mississippi where he served from 1950 until his retirement in 1971. White died on March 29, 1974.[19]

1. J. H. White, *The History of Allen-White School, 1905-1936* (Whiteville, TN: Publisher?, 1936), 4-10.
2. *A Chronicle of Black History in Hardeman County* (Bolivar, TN: Hardeman County Black History Committee, 1989), 4-6.
3. J. H. White, *The History of Allen-White School, 1905-1936* (Whiteville, TN: Publisher, 1936), 8-10.
4. J. W. Woods, "The Julius Rosenwald Fund School Building Program: A Saga in the Growth and Development of African-American Education in Selected West Tennessee Communities" (EdD diss., University of Mississippi, 1995), 176.
5. Ibid, 177
6. Ibid, 186
7. Ibid, 187
8. Ibid, 187
9. Ibid, 188
10. Ibid, 189
11. Ibid, 189
12. J. H. White, *The History of Allen-White School, 1905-1936* (Whiteville, TN: Publisher, 1937), 11- 12.
13. Berneece "What Allen-White has meant to me," *Allen-White Mirror Newspaper*, June 1937, 2.
14. J. W. Woods, "The Julius Rosenwald Fund School Building Program: A Saga in the Growth and Development of African-American Education in selected West Tennessee Communities" (EdD diss., University of Mississippi, 1995), 185.
15. Ibid, 185

16. Ibid, 185

17. F.M., et, al "NYA Students Express Appreciation for Aid," *Allen-White Mirror Newspaper*, June 1937, 2.

18. G. L. Maxwell, "Educating Youth for Citizenship," *Opportunity Journal of Negro Life*, 19, 1 (1941): 11.

19. J. W. Woods, "The Julius Rosenwald Fund School Building Program: A Saga in the Growth and Development of African-American Education in Selected West Tennessee Communities" (EdD diss., University of Mississippi, 1995), 178.

CHAPTER 6

Other Leaders

CARL SEETS

Carl L. Seets replaced White as principal of Allen-White in 1948. When Seets assumed the principalship, the school continued to expand. Under Seets' leadership, several new classrooms were built and Typing and Shorthand were added to the curriculum. Seets served for four years, from 1948 through 1952 (McKinney, 1989)

In a letter about Carl Seets by retired educator, Mabel Andrews of Bolivar, she writes:

> Mr. Seets was a native Tennessean; born in Dyer, Tennessee, but reared in McKenzie, Tennessee where he graduated from Webb High School. He received a Bachelor of Arts Degree in Social Science from Tennessee State University. He then embarked upon a teaching career in Carroll County, TN and it was during this time that he was drafted into the United States Army, World War II, and served in the South Pacific for three years, receiving an honorable discharge in 1946. This was an experience that he always alluded to with both pride and dignity. He then attended the Atlanta University School of Social Work in Atlanta, Georgia where he received a Masters Degree in Social Work.
>
> During the summer of 1948, he accepted the principalship at Allen-White High School with a tenacity and determination to make it a school of highest accreditation. He believed this could be accomplished; and with a great faith and determination, he set upon the task: So he taught through his actions the meanings of integrity, loyalty, generosity, and unselfishness. He stood for excellence for every student and for Allen-White.
>
> He was an avid reader and encouraged it. He possessed an enormous sense of curiosity and courage that allowed him to persevere and enjoy the acquisition of the Business Department, which truly enhanced the opportunities for students to obtain better and higher grades of employment. There was a chorus that he deemed second to none. His departure in 1952 carried with it dreams of an A rated Science Department.

He had a faith and was a great proponent of service to his fellowman.

Sincerely,
Mabel Andrews
March 26, 2008

MAJOR JARRETT

Major A. Jarrett took the reins of principal of Allen-White in 1952, Jarrett had attended Allen-White as a student and graduated under J. H. White's principalship. Jarrett described his return to his alma mater as follows:[1]

I had no intention of working at Allen-White. I had to sign in with the draft board and they sent me to the superintendent of education. He gave me a job and I took the job with the intention of leaving pretty soon. But I got stuck here. In the beginning I was hired in as a teacher, but before school opened, I was given the job as the principal. I had to teach a class or two but I was the principal. (Taped interview, Major Jarrett, January 21, 1995).

Under Jarrett's administration, Allen-White High School continued to expand. General Business was added and Driver Education was initiated, making Allen-White the only school in Hardeman County to offer them. Jarrett served at Allen-White until May 1970, when the schools closed due to desegregation. At the beginning of the 1970/1971 school year, former Allen-White students were bused to Bolivar or Middleton high schools. The former Allen-White Elementary School was renamed Whiteville Northside Elementary School. Jarrett continued as principal of Whiteville Northside until retirement in 1979. Mckinney wrote this as a brief epilogue of the history of Allen-White School:[2]

> Thus closes the historical account of Allen-White
> High School, the institution which began in 1905,
> in the Old Masonic Lodge Hall as Jesse C. Allen's
> School for Colored Children. Let it be noted, however
> that societal reality easily closes historical accounts,
> but the influence of an educational institution is less
> easily determined (McKinney, 1989, p.7).

Allen-White Elementary School

During the school year 1966/1967, Allen-White Elementary School was formed. Grades K-6 were divided from the high school and a separate administration was formed for their management and supervision. C. Elma Motley, Whiteville native and long-time educator, was appointed principal of Allen-White Elementary School. Motley had been principal of Union Springs Elementary School for many years prior to being appointed to Allen-White Elementary. Motley was highly respected for her leadership and commitment to the education of boys and girls in this community.

Upon Motley's retirement in 1969, Evelyn C. Robertson Jr. was appointed principal of Allen-White Elementary for the school year 1969/1970.

The 1970/1971 school year was the first year for full desegregation of Hardeman County schools. Robertson was assigned to Central High School in Bolivar as vice-principal for the 1970/1971 school year. He served in this role until 1974.

Though idle as an institution, the history of Allen-White looms large in the lives of those past and present. The lives of those that this institution shaped will continue, as history is still being written and the proud past of this school is further etched into the annals of education history and the history of this county.

1. J. W. Woods, "The Julius Rosenwald Fund School Building Program: A Saga in the Growth and Development of African-American Education in Selected West Tennessee Communities" (EdD diss., University of Mississippi, 1995), 179.
2. Ibid, 180

CHAPTER 7

The Role of the Julius Rosenwald Foundation

From 1910 into the early 1930s, more than fifty-three hundred buildings were constructed in African American communities throughout fifteen southern states. Seed money came from Chicago philanthropist Julius Rosenwald, CEO of Sears Roebuck & Company. Black communities put up cash and local school boards agreed to operate the facilities.[1]

The Rosenwald schools blossomed from a problem and a partnership. The problem was the sorry state of African American education in the South after 1900. Since slavery times, when most states had flatly forbidden teaching slaves to read, black Americans had hungered for learning. They flocked to academies set up by missionaries after the Civil War, and poured into public schools in the late nineteenth century, often attending in larger numbers than their white counterparts.

The separate schools for blacks were never equal, but things got worse after 1900. That was when southern states stripped blacks of the right to vote—disenfranchisement. In 1915, the U.S. average spent per pupil for education was $30 per student. The amount for blacks was a mere fraction of that. In Tennessee, the amount spent per black pupil was less than $10.

In 1910, an unlikely partnership took aim at the problem. The idea man was a black ex-slave in Alabama. Booker T. Washington headed Tuskegee Institute, which he built into a major black college by convincing northern philanthropists to aid a hands-on self-approach he called "industrial education." Washington thought that self-help and northern philanthropy might transform public schools as well. In 1913, he found his angel in Julius Rosenwald.

Rosenwald was a white Northerner and a German-Jewish immigrant's son raised in Springfield, Illinois. He joined a fledging Chicago store named Sears Roebuck & Company in 1897. By 1909, he was CEO of the world's largest retailer.

Rosenwald turned energetically to philanthropy. He quickly became known for thoughtful gifts that reached far beyond Chicago. He gave $1000 grants to the first one hundred counties to hire county extension agents, helping the U.S. Department of Agriculture launch a program that still shapes rural America today. Noting the thousands of African American's fleeing the South, he helped build almost two dozen black YMCAs to provide lodging and social services in America's largest cities.

Rosenwald's religious heritage gave him a particular affinity for African Americans, according to grandson and biographer Dr. Peter Ascoli.

Booker T. Washington's vision of rural schools caught Rosenwald's imagination. Together, the idea man and the money man hammered out an early example of a now common philanthropic tool—the matching grant. If a rural black community could scrape together a contribution, and if the white school board would agree to operate the facility, Rosenwald would contribute cash, usually about 1/5 of the total project. The aim was quite radical, a Rosenwald Fund official later wrote—"Not merely a series of schoolhouses, but a community enterprise in cooperation between citizen and officials, White and Colored." Even Professor W.E.B. Dubois, the great rival of Booker T. Washington, applauded the Rosenwald initiative. Dubois focused his own energies on college education to produce black leaders, and when Julius Rosenwald died in 1932, Dubois penned a lengthy appreciation of the philanthropist's impact on pre-college opportunities.[2]

Work-a-day African Americans enthusiastically embraced Rosenwald's school construction plans, even though it meant considerable sacrifice on top of taxes they were already paying. Cash was scarce in this region where many farmed "on shares." To gather nickels and dimes, women of a community might hold a "box party," fixing boxed lunches on which neighbors could bid. Families joined to plant an acre of cotton or raise hogs and chickens to be sold for the effort. Blacks who owned land might donate the school site, or cut trees to be sawn into boards for work crews.

Soon, schools dotted the South. By 1932, when the construction grants ended, 5357 new buildings stood in 883 counties throughout fifteen southern states. Most were schools, but workshops and teachers homes also received funding. Tennessee boasted 373 of these buildings.

The Rosenwald Fund provided state of the art architectural plans. Two black architecture professors at Tuskegee, Robert R. Taylor and W. A. Hazel, drew the first set for a 1915 pamphlet. In 1920, Rosenwald official Samuel L. Smith assumed the task. His *Community School Plans Pattern* books were eventually distributed by the Interstate School Building Service and reached thousands of communities far beyond the South.

Large banks of windows characterized Rosenwald schools, a simple but powerful innovation in an era when electricity seldom reached into rural areas. Designers carefully specified room size and height, blackboard and desk placement, paint colors, and even the arrangements of window shades in order to make the best use of natural light.

Inside, the buildings almost always included meeting space, a key aspect of Booker T. Washington's vision. In smaller buildings, a moveable partition allowed classrooms to be thrown together as an assembly hall. Bigger schools featured a permanent auditorium. Dr. Washington saw each school as a community center. Rosenwald buildings would not only teach the young, but would help dispersed people come together to improve farming techniques and forge strong community culture. Indeed, families often built homes clustered around the schools, creating settlements that persist today.

According to Mary Hoffschwelle, a history professor at Middle Tennessee State University, "In their heyday, Rosenwald schools accounted for one in five black schools in the South." She stated that Rosenwald's was one of the most significant initiatives in African American public education before Brown.[3]

At a time of limited educational opportunities for black students, Rosenwald schools filled a crucial need. Existing schools were crowded, housed in buildings such as churches or barns, and did not provide secondary education.

Rosenwald schools, which were built with a combination of grants, local taxes, and black money and labor "made a huge difference in the lives of individuals there," according to John Hildreth, director of the National Trust for Historic Preservation's Southern Office. "It made the best of a bad situation."[4]

It was the initiative and the energy of Booker T. Washington, with the financial support of Julius Rosenwald, that aided blacks, despite racial barriers of reconstruction and,Jim Crowism. Washington was not just an educator, he was an accomplished self-help advocate and strong proponent of black economic independence.

1. Tom Hancett, "Beacons for Black Education in the American South," Rosenwald Schools, http://www.rosenwaldplans.org (posted 02/24/2006).
2. Tom Hancett, "Saving the South's Rosenwald Schools," Rosenwald Schools, http://www.rosenwaldplans.org/history.html (posted 02/24/2006).
3. "School's Historic ties to an unequal past", Orlando Sentinenel. Com.http://www.orlando sentinel.com/bal_te.md.schoolhouse 17 May,01633791.story page 1 (posted 2/24/2006) 37.
4. Ibid, 1

CHAPTER 8

Community Fundraising Support and Structure

1929 Mortgage Burning –Thanksgiving Day 1929

Grassroots support was a critical ingredient for the success of the Rosenwald School Building Program. A shared faith in the power of self-help let Booker T. Washington and Julius Rosenwald insist on local contributions to match the amount of a Rosenwald Grant, rather than insisting on full public or philanthropic funding. They believed that personal sacrifices of hard-earned cash, lumber, and labor would strengthen rural African American's commitment to their communities. In practice, the self-help requirements made rural African Americans the driving force behind the Rosenwald Program and the arbiters of its meaning for southern communities.

Local African American leaders, teachers, principals, school trustees, ministers, and successful farm or business owners often initiated building campaigns. They wrote to the state education departments, the Tuskegee Institute, and the Rosenwald Fund for information, lobbied county superintendents and school boards for additional funding, and recruited their fellow citizens' support.

To make their matching contribution, school patrons organized themselves into committees to find and buy the land, to cut trees and saw the lumber for the school, to haul the building materials to the school site, and sometimes even to build the schools themselves. Those who pledged contributions of money and labor included rural wage earners such as sawmill and domestic workers, farm owners and tenants, and the members of church congregations and fraternal lodges. Some donated a day's pay, or the proceeds of an acre of cotton; others sold chickens. School rallies, community picnics, and entertainment brought in cash as well. The result was a school building that stood as a tangible expression of community determination to provide a decent education for its children.

Organization was a distinct trademark of J. H. White, principal of Allen-White School. Fundraising success and effectiveness was the direct result of his effort to organize the communities in groups, creating competition in order to meet funding benchmarks. Thanksgiving rallies culminated funding drives on an annual basis. The timing of Thanksgiving was not coincidental; since most of the citizens were farmers, sharecroppers, tenants, and so on, this timing coincided with the harvest season—a time when citizens would likely have some expendable funds. For many years, the Thanksgiving rallies created buzz in the communities throughout Hardeman County and represented opportunities for citizens to take pride in contributing to the school's financial needs, thus aiding their children in their quest for education.

Through the efforts of the Parent-Teacher Association, $5,172.44 was raised between 1929/30. In 1929, the organization paid off the $1724 note on the administration building, additionally, $800 was targeted to pay on the fifteen room girl's dormitory and teachers home.

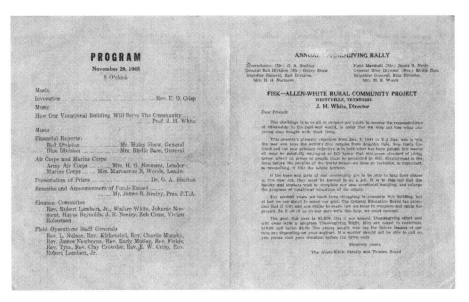

The girl's dormitory and teachers' home (Ingram Hall) was a colonial frame structure costing $4000. To carry out this project, a note was secured at the Whiteville Bank for $2500. The men that signed the note included the trustee board: Wm. Murphy, chairman; Dr. G. A. Shelton, secretary; Crawford Robertson, treasurer; S.W.J. Allen; Jim

Reynolds; Frank Baird; and E. Crisp. Guarantors included, J. H. White, A. E. Lockert, Johnnie Norment, Simon Norment, Tin Crowder, Sam Murphy, Johnny Parram, Joe Harris, Charlie Cox, Will McNeal, Charlie Stallings, Lewis Morrow, Vivian Robertson, Charlie Lewis, Clift Rhodes, Montry Robertson, Finas Newborn, Billie Haynes, Jessie Bufford, Jim Neely, T. G. White, Stokes Crowder, and George McGuire.[1]

The 1930/1931 Thanksgiving rally raised $800. Support came from friends in and out of state. The rally was divided into five divisions, namely: the church conference, which was made up of men; the tTouring party, which was made up of women; teachers; trustees; and the Mutt and Jeff campaign, which was made up of the student body. Men were asked for $5 each. Women were asked for $3 each. Teachers were asked to raise $15. Trustees were asked to raise $15, and students were asked to solicit as much as possible.

The 1941 Thanksgiving effort raised $1500 for Cheek Hall, which contained the new gymnasium. Fourteen rally leaders and their disciples reported overwhelming success. The Thanksgiving program began with a singing contest at 2:30 PM at which singing groups from all neighboring communities contested for the $10 prizes offered. Mr. S. H. Wells was master of ceremonies.

All of the Whiteville community was alive. From every surrounding road, throngs were gathered, in wagons, ox carts, on horseback, or on foot. After an afternoon of music, refreshments, and fun, the many friends of Allen-White filled the auditorium eagerly awaiting the "final count." The fourteen rally leaders and their disciples each reported that their efforts had been met with overwhelming success.

At the end of the ceremony, Mr. J. H. White, supervising principal, rendered a stirring address in which he expressed thanks and congratulations to all contributing service toward the education of African American boys and girls in Hardeman County.

Prizes were awarded to the highest individual solicitors, Mrs. A. C. White won the $15 first prize, she raised $243.36. Second prize, a "loving cup," was awarded to Mrs. G. W. Wells for the patron raising the most money. She raised $27.50. A $10 third prize went to the student raising the highest amount of money. Hazel Bowles, raised $33.75.[2]

The fourteen group leaders reports and amounts were as follows:

Group one – Leader M. B. Woods, disciple Zebedee Cross, amount $126.02.

Group two – Leader Mrs. A. C. White, disciple E. R. Shockley, amount $243.36

Group three – Leader H. G. Norment, disciple Robert Motley, amount $182.83.

Group four – Leader M. L. Robertson, disciple Huley Shaw, amount $106.05

Group five – Leader W. R. Woods, disciple, Johnson Mays, amount $101.05

Group six – Leader D. R. Reed, disciple G. A. Shelton, amount $106.40

Group seven – Leader M. C. White, disciple Johnnie Garrett, amount $89.10

Group eight – Leader W. D. Greene, disciple James R. Neely, amount $50.

Group nine – Leader S. E. Procter, disciple William Haynes, amount $106.75

Group ten – Leader R. L. McArthur, disciple William Harris, amount $104.60.

Professor J. H. White, amount $474.00

F. D. Fant, amount $69.75. [3]

In order to prepare for the Thanksgiving Day rally, each trustee was assigned an area to solicit funds. Each would travel to that area, solicit pledges, and report them at the rally. Trustee Crawford Robertson was assisted in his work by his daughter, Myrtle Robertson, who described her father's effort.[4]

I would go with my daddy. My daddy couldn't write, but he could talk and I would write names down and the amounts they promised to give. We rode in a buggy, driving his favorite horse and I enjoyed that. (Taped interview, February 11, 1995)

Robertson also recalled her father's desire for the enhancement of education, as she related:[5]

When the first load of lumber came to build the school, they did not have
the money to pay for it. I remember that Mr. Allen came out to talk to my
daddy to let him have $600 to pay for it. Finally, my daddy told him that he
would. He left flying, trying to get to town on time to tell them.

To support the massive building and development of the Allen-White High School further in the late thirties and early forties, the Allen-White Rural Community Center, Inc. was formed. Trustees of the center consisted of:

R. P. Bass – Whiteville	Ben Murphy – Somerville
F. T. Blalock – Whiteville	Whit Nelms- Bolivar
E. W. Crisp – Vildo	Jim Neely- Whiteville
Webb Deen – Whiteville	Johnny Norment- Whiteville
C. R. Howse – Whiteville	Vivian Robertson – Whiteville
Attorney E. J. Harris – Whiteville	Dr. George N. Redd – Nashville
Dr. Almont Mitchell – Whiteville	Dr. G. A. Shelton – Whiteville
Robert Motley – Whiteville	W. E. Turner – Nashville

(See Appendix for funds raised by the Allen-White P.T.A.)

Various organizational approaches were used to facilitate fund raising. In the 1945 annual rally, divisions were headed by a general and a brigadier general. As late as 1959/60, groups for fund raising included Beavers, Trojans, and Victory Clubs. Known leaders of these clubs were Norman Rhodes, Beavers; Zeb Cross, Victory; and Galveston Woods, Trojans.

The "box supper" was a poplar community fundraiser. Johnnie Curtis, a 1933 Allen-White graduate and faculty member, described the box supper as follows:[7]

> A box supper was when you would get as many ladies in the community to fix a box of food, and the ladies would choose so many men to eat from her box, and they'd pay her so much money. We would meet at the school

and I'd be over at my table with my men and my basket, and the next one would be at the next table, and so on. Sometimes, the men folk would want to get some food from the other tables, but they had to stay at their own tables. The average box supper would bring about ten to fifteen dollars, depending on how much you charged. In my box, I always had a vegetable, greens, peas, or beans, and I had chicken, rolls, pickles, and cake. The food didn't spoil then like it does today. (Taped interview, January 21, 1995)

The community also showed its support to the Allen-White Laugh and Minstrel Show. The activity garnered outstanding community support as well as revenue for the school buildings and maintenance program. Alfreeda Lake McKinney tells of her experience as a participant in the Minstrel Show.[8]

The minstrel show was a take-off, I guess, on the black-face minstrels that we've heard about way back. This was a group of students that were selected by faculty and music teachers to take part in a minstrel show. We would have maybe eight boys and ten or twelve girls. O this group, we would have the "end men," who were comedians, and the girls were the chorus girls, and in the center of this was one who served as the "interlocutor." He was the one posed the questions and sorta kept the show running. The girls dressed in very pretty evening clothes. The interlocutor would have on a suit, maybe an improvised tuxedo and a top hat, and the end men were there in black face that would be in street clothes, farm clothes, or whatever. The interlocutor would ask questions to the end men and they would answer with some comedic joke or some tale. At intervals, the girls would sing too, I was the interlocutor at one time and they dressed me up like a man. This group would perform at Whiteville School, at schools in the county, just traveling on the old bus. When the basketball team would take trips out of time, the minstrel show would go along with them; we would have the basketball game one night and the minstrel show the next night. We were received well. We'd have packed houses. (Taped interview, January 24, 1995)

Another example of community support was when the Whiteville Community was without electricity, the local farmers agreed to furnish the thirty-five foot chestnut poles to meet the electricity company's specifications in order to bring electricity to the school.

The PTA also took total financial responsibility for building three buildings on the Allen-White campus—the gymnasium, the sandwich shop, and the boy's dormitory.

1. Author and title? *Hardeman County Mirror Newspaper*, May 1930, 4.
2. J.H. White. "$1500 Raised for Hall", *Allen-White Voice Newspaper*, November 28, 1941, 1.
3. I bid, 4,5
4. J. W. Woods, "The Julius Rosenwald Fund School Building Program: A Saga in the Growth and Development of African-American Education in selected West Tennessee Communities" (EdD diss., University of Mississippi, 1995), 182.
5. Ibid, 182
6. J. W. Woods, "The Julius Rosenwald Fund School Building Program: A Saga in the Growth and Development of African-American Education in selected West Tennessee Communities," (EdD diss., University of Mississippi, 1995), 183.
7. Ibid, 184

CHAPTER 9

Notable Graduates

Many graduates of Allen-White were inspired to pursue education as their chosen field of work. Many returned to their alma mater to teach or to assume administrative positions. Some of these included Johnnie G. Curtis, Major Jarrett, Minerva Jarrett, John Brady, Arthur Harris, Alice Fentress Ferguson, Dorothy Rainier, Marie Cobb Wisdom, Georgia Bass Crowder, Glorious Bass Holmes, Hugholene Ellison Robertson, Evelyn C. Robertson Jr., Nannie S. Pratt, Samuel Bufford, Willie Golden, Jesse I. Norment, Shirlie Greene, Henry Woods, Surleaster C. Maclin, Mabel McKinnie Andrews, Jeff E. McKinnie, Lorenzo Bufford, Leonard Black, Bernice Dawkins Stallings, Rebecca Davis Lewis, Gladys Davis Jimmerson, Earnest Wilburn, Jesse C. Rhodes, Clora A. Horton, Elsie Wilkes, Lillie B. Rivers, Martha Jo Pirtle, Joe R. White, and Doris Reynolds.

Other graduates chose teaching as a career. Some worked in Hardeman County, some throughout the state, and others in other parts of the country. Some even include college professors. This list includes Ruby McKinnie, Frankie Hamer Hicks, Earnest C. Rhodes, Georgia R. Hunter, Ora Mae Herron Allen, Mary Willis Griffin, Earnestine Rivers

Henderson, Earnestine Lake Bills, Josie Cobb Bryant, Tom Cobb, Marie Murphy, Neola W. Sardon, Dorothy Walton Joy, Jacob Cox, Katie Hamer Lake, Johnny Lake, Lucille Anderson Leach, Dora Anderson, Daniel Bufford, Ocie Johnson, Charles J. Johnson, Jerry McKinnie, James Perry, Agatha Lake, Mattie Brewer, Willie Crisp, Monroe Hussey, Benonie Harris, Marie Harris Croom, Nora Lake Harwell, Mary Fason James, Josie McNeal, Usley Woods, Gladia McGuire Perry, Marilyn J. Rivers Morrow, Marilyn Perry Smith, Jessie Allen Boyle, Opal L. Franklin, Bobbie L. Pettis, Elizabeth L. Hills, Shirley Crowder, Irene W. Herron, Roberta Bass Wilkes, Annie D. Holmes, James Scott, Fredell Harris, Anna Hodges, Ruth Strayhorn, Eve R. Horton, Noah Jones, Jesse Harvey, Desiree D. Walker, Dorothy Dotson, John Greene, Mabel Parham, Alice Parham, Floyd White, Gertrude Person, Earnestine Dotson, Dorothy Tisdale, Nellie Stewart, Eroy Beard, Juanita Cox, Charlene Groves, William McNeal, Will W. Scott, Esther B. Harris, Dorothy N. Perry, Lizzie M. McGuire, Doris Grimes, Georgia M. Campbell, Lloyd Norment, Annie L. Hudson, Edith Shockley Wolfrey, Margaret H. Wade, Pauline Woods, James Murphy, Geneva Jordan, Eula M. Finley, Theodore Woods, Spencer Davis, Velma Beard Glass, Inez Bonds, Geneva B. Woods, Lewis Wiley, Major Wilburn, Lacie Murphy Cousins, Gaston Andrews, William Jones, Mamie R. Parham Anderson, Edward Worthy, Joyce Spencer, J. A. Robertson, Lucy Bell Crowder Boone, Henry Lee Woods and Ruby Polk Ruffin.

One graduate, Earnest C. Rhodes, served as a distinguished sociology professor at Tennessee State University in Nashville, Tennessee. Charles Johnson served as director of schools in Hardeman County. Mack Scott had a distinguished career as a veterinarian and researcher at Meharry Medical College in Nashville, Tennessee. Alfreeda Lake McKinney served as supervisor of instruction for the Hardeman County School System. Major Wilburn served as director of chapter programs for the Hardeman County School System.

Former student Johnny W. Shaw is currently serving as a member of the Tennessee State Legislature. Willie Earl Spencer is currently serving as mayor of Hardeman County. Odell Horton has served as an attorney, Memphis city administrator, Lemoyne -Owen College president, and a federal judge. Shirley Greene became a dentist. Earl White earned a law degree. Donald Pitts became a lawyer and judge. Ezell Dawkins earned a law degree and served as a College Board Member in California.

Several former students or graduates made their careers with the U.S. Postal Service including Glenn Dotson, George T. Dotson, Patricia B. Jackson, and Cosette Johnson Crawford.

Many graduates of Allen-White pursued careers in the agricultural industry, becoming teachers, extension agents, conservationists, researchers, scientists, and so on. This was very natural since farming and agriculture was the predominant occupation in this area at one time. Some that pursued this field include Odell Greene, Willie McKinnie, J. W. McGuire, Haston Neely, Bill Miller, Robert L. McKinnie, Benjamin Crowder, Arthur Harris, Leonard Black, Johnny Lake, James Herron, Arthur Williams, Rayphield Murphy, Lorenzo Tisdale, Roscoe Mays Jr., Roosevelt Perry, George Prewitt and Lewis Wiley.

Home economics graduates include Hortense Ferguson Parham, Essie Prewitt, Dorothy M. Lofton, and Minerva Jarrett.

Several graduates are also business owners. Opal J. Shaw and Johnny Shaw are owners of Shaw Broadcasting Company, in Bolivar, and Opal's Restaurant. The Shaws also are gospel recording artists. Thomas Scott is a very successful businessman in California. Jimmy L. Robertson and Ray Bufford are owners of barbering establishments. Darnell Robertson, who worked for New York Life Insurance Company for more than forty years, is currently serving as a councilman in Warrensville, Ohio. L. T. Boyle served as a technician/repairman for South Central Bell/Bell South. He currently owns and operates his own telephone and electric service in Bolivar. Nylon Holloway worked as a technician/repairman for AT&T in Cleveland Ohio. Walter C. Bowden owns Bolivar Cleaners in Bolivar. Delois R. Wright is the owner of Wright Way Travel Agency in Columbus, Ohio. Rayphield Wiley is a retired brick mason in Whiteville. Mozell Greer is a businessman in Ohio.

Nurses have included Ruthie Willis Hawkins, Katherine B. Boyd, Christine W. Posey, Ocie D. Holmes, Rose Norment Harris, Lois N. Harris, Dulvet Harris, Willa Mae Toone, and Dorothy Scott. Cleaster K. Sain is a licensed occupational therapist. Dr. Thomas E. Motley, even though not a graduate, got his early education at Allen-White and is a highly recognized internist in Memphis, Tennessee. Jewel Bell became a Veterinarian.

Opal Dotson Hennings became a licensed clinical social worker; she also taught social work at Murray State University in Kentucky. Madison Shockley became a licensed social worker, actor, activist, and author. Margaret Robertson became a licensed social worker. Marilyn Wiley McKinnie served as a social worker. James A. Robertson is a juvenile probations officer, and Desiree Dotson Walker is an author.

Former students and graduates that pursued the ministry and became pastors include Charlie R. Boyd, Jerry Crisp, Jesse E. Williams, Arthur Lee Dotson, Robert Parham, Percy Hunter, William Bufford, Johnny Shaw, Benjamin Bell, Charles Rainer, Joshua Newborn, Corrine Robinson and K. C. Sain. In politics, William Sidney Woods has served as alderman and vice mayor of Whiteville for many years. George T. Dotson served as alderman in Whiteville and aspired for the mayor's office. Jimmy L. Robertson is currently serving as alderman in Whiteville. Opal J. Shaw and Major Wilburn serve on the Hardeman County Commission, and Charles E. Ellison is serving as alderman in Toone, Tennessee.

Numerous graduates and former students made careers in the Military, some had careers in the steel mills of the North, and others made careers in the automobile industry.

As impressive as this list is, it is certainly not exhaustive. Allen-White's sons and daughters have successfully pursued careers in every field of human endeavor. I apologize for any omissions, for Allen-White's graduates are found in all corners of this country and abroad.

CHAPTER 10

Conclusion

In recent years, much interest has been demonstrated in the history and legacy of former Rosenwald schools such as Allen-White. In November of 2008, the Fox television station in Memphis, Tennessee did a two-part series on the history and legacy of the former Woodstock High School in Lucy, Tennessee.

ANN SMITHWICK & EVELYN ROBERTSON

Please join us for the opening reception of

Rosenwald Revisted

WISDOM FROM THE ELDERS

WITH PHOTOGRAPHY BY ANN SMITHWICK

FRIDAY NIGHT JANUARY 5TH, 5:30 PM

BRIEF SPEAKER SERIES, 6:30 PM

WITH DR. PETER ASCOLI, MARY HOFFSCHWELLE,
MRS. IDA PALMER, MR. EVELYN ROBERTSON

NATIONAL CIVIL RIGHTS MUSEUM

450 MULBERRY STREET
MEMPHIS, TN 38103

EXHIBIT DATES: JANUARY 5TH - MARCH 15TH

PLEASE RESPOND
901.521.9699 EXT 233
WWW.CIVILRIGHTSMUSEUM.ORG

In 2005, the author was contacted by Ann Smithwick, a professional photographer from Memphis, Tennessee whose family purchased, renovated, and converted a former Rosenwald school in Braden, Tennessee into their residence. After moving there and finding out the history of the school from the neighbors, she became very interested and wanted to know more about Rosenwald schools. She attended a restoration conference at Fisk University in Nashville, Tennessee, which dealt with the history of these schools and examples of restorative efforts. It was through attendance at this conference that the author's name was introduced to her, as Allen-White School had been placed on the state and national register of historic places. She followed up, and initiated contact. Her interests were to use her photographic skills, using an old method of photography to photograph former students and graduates. Through this initiative, a video was also produced about the school. The pictures were used in an exhibit, entitled "Rosenwald Revisited: Wisdom from the Elders," which went on display at the National Civil Rights Museum in Memphis, Tennessee for three months. Ann Smithwick was responsible for this exhibit. Besides her photographs, the exhibit was comprised of memorabilia, class pictures, and other artifacts from the Allen-White School. At the exhibit's grand opening ceremony, Dr. Peter Ascoli, grandson of Julius Rosenwald was present. Ann met Dr. Ascoli at the Fisk Conference. He shared much about his grandfather's commitment and desire to see that African American youth throughout the South had educational opportunities. Dr. Ascoli has written a scholarly book about his grandfather and his philanthropic pursuits.

EVELYN ROBERTSON & DR. PETER ASCOLI

At the opening ceremony, the author was asked to give remarks (see remarks at the end of the book). This exhibit was attended by thousands of citizens from the mid-South.

In 2008, the Hardeman County chapter of the Association for the Preservation of Tennessee Antiquities requested that the Allen-White exhibit be housed at the Little Courthouse Museum in Bolivar, Tennessee. It was on display there from February through April of 2008.

Several hundred local citizens were able to view the exhibit; many were inspired as well as informed. For some, it brought back fond memories. Cissye Pierce, president of the local APTA chapter was instrumental in this initiative and secured a grant from the Tennessee Humanities to support its sponsorship. She and other APTA members strongly supported this effort.

As a result of the exhibit at the Little Courthouse, Camille Shavon Hudson, a salon owner and writer for an African American newspaper, was inspired (by a photograph of the 1940-41 Allen-White girl's national championship basketball team that had been victorious at Tuskegee Institute in Alabama in 1940/1941) to coordinate a successful effort to recognize the five surviving members of the team. An event called "A Victory Celebration" was held November 23, 2008 at Antioch Baptist Church to recognize the team. One former player, Georgia McKinnie Campbell, then eighty-four years old, returned from Spartanburg, South Carolina. Emma Tynes Harris, in her mid-eighties, returned from Chicago, Illinois. And, three local team members, Marie Brady, Emma D. Herron Lake Lanier, and Beatrice Woods Spencer were there. Over three hundred people attended this event. These ladies each had success in their chosen fields. My remarks at this event are included in the appendix.

WKNO, an NPR radio station in Memphis, Tennessee conducted an interview with the author in 2007 regarding the Allen-White School and its history.

Though the doors were closed at the Allen-White School in 1970, its legacy lives, as demonstrated on a daily basis through the lives of its many graduates and former students. The recent interest in its history is further vindication of the foresight of its founders and the vision and insight that they had about the possibilities of shaping raw human beings into viable, creditable, intelligent, productive citizens. I hope and pray that the current and future generations of young African Americans can learn from the sacrifices, failures, persevering, and successes of these pioneers who were visionary in every respect.

12/27/07

Dear Evelyn,

I can't thank you enough for sharing your story, and that of Allen-White School, with me. What a legacy. I hope to hear soon that plans are underway for the museum there at Allen-White. Please stay in touch.

Happy New Year!

Sarah

NPR for the Mid-South
WKNO-FM 91.1/Memphis • WKNP-FM 90.1/Jackson, TN

It is my dream that one day, a permanent home will be available to house the many artifacts and memorabilia of this historic institution, where current and future generations will share its history.

As this chapter comes to an end, the story is still being written on Allen-White School, as long as graduates and former students are still making contributions to society and the world in general. The time and effort devoted to this project has been long and arduous, but there are no regrets; it has been time well spent. The author is grateful to those that shared information in response to the many questions. To those that encouraged me, I will be forever grateful.

May the memory of Allen-White School live on!

APPENDIX

Allen-White High School Alma Mater
According to Jesse C. Rhodes, former faculty member at Allen-White, A. C. Williams, former agriculture instructor at Allen-White, and former WDIA radio station personality, penned the words to the Allen-White Alma Mater. It is sung to the tune "Amici."

The words are as follows:

Hail to thee our Alma Mater,
colors white and blue (colors
white and blue).

Allen-White thy sons and daughters
ever will be true.

Chorus
Grateful, loyal, true, and faithful
we will ever be (we will ever be).
May thy name be everlasting 'til
eternity.

When the days of joy and
laughter fade upon thy sight
(fade upon thy sight),
we will love our Alma Mater
dear old Allen-White.

Fight Songs

Allen-White Bears are on the floor.
Allen-White Bears are ready to go.
Allen-White Bears will 'beat' and so
Beware – Beware – Beware

Just as soon as the game begins,
then you'll know we're sure to win.
Allen-White Bears will never give in.
Give in – Give in – Give in.

Day is breakin' and the good ole' sun is shinin'
Allen-White Bears got the Woodstock Aggies'
Whinin!
What's the matter with 'em? Whinin!
What are they whinin' 'bout? Whinin!
Whinin! Whinin! Whinin!

New Farmers of America State Champions

Arthur F. Harris, Advisor

James Hunter '60 – Seed Identification

Abb B. Jones '60 – Soil Identification

Laston Jones '60 – Public Speaking

Willie McKinnie '64 Dairy Judging

Bill Miller '60 Beef Cattle Judging

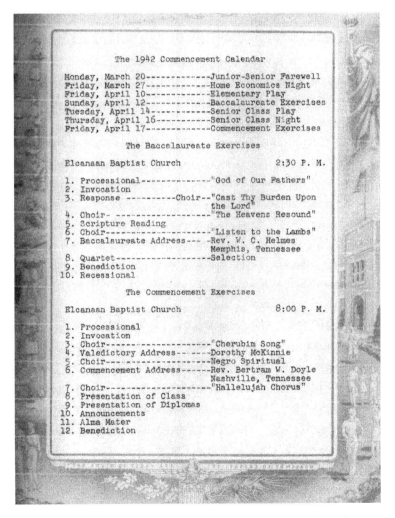

The 1942 Commencement Calendar

Monday, March 20-------------Junior-Senior Farewell
Friday, March 27-------------Home Economics Night
Friday, April 10-------------Elementary Play
Sunday, April 12-------------Baccalaureate Exercises
Tuesday, April 14------------Senior Class Play
Thursday, April 16-----------Senior Class Night
Friday, April 17-------------Commencement Exercises

The Baccalaureate Exercises

Elcanaan Baptist Church   2:30 P. M.

1. Processional--------------"God of Our Fathers"
2. Invocation
3. Response ----------Choir--"Cast Thy Burden Upon
the Lord"
4. Choir- ------------------"The Heavens Resound"
5. Scripture Reading
6. Choir--------------------"Listen to the Lambs"
7. Baccalaureate Address--- -Rev. W. C. Helmes
Memphis, Tennessee
8. Quartet------------------Selection
9. Benediction
10. Recessional

The Commencement Exercises

Elcanaan Baptist Church   8:00 P. M.

1. Processional
2. Invocation
3. Choir--------------------"Cherubim Song"
4. Valedictory Address-- ----Dorothy McKinnie
5. Choir---------------------Negro Spiritual
6. Commencement Address------Rev. Bertram W. Doyle
Nashville, Tennessee
7. Choir--------------------"Hallelujah Chorus"
8. Presentation of Class
9. Presentation of Diplomas
10. Announcements
11. Alma Mater
12. Benediction

NATIONAL REGISTER OF HISTORIC PLACES

In 2004, Allen-White School was nominated for designation as a State and National Historic Site by the Tennessee Historic Commission. This designation was awarded by the U.S. Department of Interior in September of 2004. Support for this nomination was provided by the Center for Preservation from Middle Tennessee State University. Dr. Carroll Van West was instrumental in the application preparation and its ultimate designation. A huge debt of gratitude is owed to Dr. Van West.

The Allen-White School was eligible for the National Register of Historic Places under Criterion A for its statewide significance in education. The application included many of the historical facts cited by the author in this book. Unique features of the application were the funding of the school compared to other Rosenwald Schools in Tennessee and the significant local association with African-American citizens of Hardeman County. The unselfishness of citizens to make financial sacrifices for their children was very much a part of the application narrative. In one portion of the narrative Dr. Van West referred to a Farmer that reportedly had pledged $100 each year so long as the demand for the school warranted it. The Farmer was later identified as Crawford Robertson, Grandfather of the author who was also the treasurer of the fundraising campaign.

The National Register of Historic Places is the nation's official list of cultural resources worthy of preservation. It is part of a nationwide program that coordinates and supports efforts to identify, evaluate and protect historic resources. The Tennessee Historic Commission administers the program in Tennessee.

ADMINISTRATION

To our graduates who are leaving Allen-White, our best wishes go with you for your success.

Let us keep aware that with all privileges goes a responsibility. Therefore, take your future assignments seriously and make the most of each opportunity.

M. A. Jarrett, Principal

Past

Present

Alma Mater

```
Hail to thee our Alma Mater
Colors white and blue (Colors white and blue)
Allen-White thy sons and daughters
Ever will be true.

            Chorus

Grateful, loyal, true, and faithful
We will ever be (We will ever be)
May thy name be everlasting
'Till eternity.

When the days of joy and laughter
Fade upon thy sight (Fade upon thy sight)
We will love our Alma Mater
Dear old Allen-White.
```

Future

Mont Woods

Earnest Greer

Sam Hamer

Boys Basketball Team

Louis Wiley

Worda Sain-Daniel Clark

James Jones

Paul Hickman-Arthur Harris

Mont-Sam

Donors To
Cheek Hall Fund

Mr. J. H. White and faculty submit the following names of donors to our Thanksgiving Rally. We are sincerely grateful to you for making Cheek Hall a reality.

Prof. J. H. White

J. H. White	$5.00
Mr. Frank Hay, Little Rock Ark	1.00
Miss Mobes K. Howell, Scarrett College, Nashville	5.00
Colonial Baking Co.	5.00
Thomas J. Powers, Jr.	5.00
Mrs. Katherine Allen	25.00
American Snuff Co.	25.00
Orgill Brothers	25.00
Mrs. W. I. Webb	25.00
Mr. J. C. Reaves	3.00
Mr. W. B. Chase	350.00

Group 1 — M. B. Woods
Mr. Zebedee Cross

Mrs. G. W. Wells	$27.50
Mr. Zebedee Cross	7.00
Mr. Bethel McNeal	5.00
Mrs. Murvarene Woods	5.00
Miss Lous Caruthers	1.00
Mr. J. W. Wilson	1.00
Mr. J. Bishop	1.00
Mr. Robert Spencer	1.00
Mr. Joe Bowers	1.00
Mr. Tom Crowder	1.00
Mrs. C. Elmer Motley	3.00
Prof. Earnest Rivers	2.50
Miss Bessie Walton	3.00
Mr. Henry Perry	2.00
Mr. Walter Wilks	1.00
Mr. Mathis Rhodes	2.50
Mr. Shan Woods	2.00
Mr. Herman McKinney	2.50
Mrs. Bernice Reaves	1.50
Mrs. Rosie Bell Reynolds	2.00
Mrs. Rosie Bell Woods	1.00
Mrs. Ida Harris	3.00
Mrs. Mary Lou Crowder	1.00
Miss Frances Spencer	1.00
Thomas Baker	3.00
Ollie M. Bufford	1.60
Vuleria Miller	4.50
James Davis	2.00
Essie Wiley	1.35
Magnolia Murphy	3.60
Blanche Traylor	1.80
Johnnie M. Douglass	4.52
Robert Beard	1.00
William Sydney Woods	1.00
Essie Beard	1.50

Group 2 — Mrs. J. H. White
Mr. E. R. Shockley

Mrs. J. H. White	$5.00
Hohn Whitlow	1.00
Edison Shockley	1.65
Wardie Sain	1.50
Alton Jarmon	1.50
Gertrude Woods	2.70
Autre Newborne	3.00
Mary E. Ashcraft	3.35

Minerva Norment	3.00
Levell Motley	5.00
Lawyer Bert Hodge	5.00
Mr. R. E. Clay	5.00
Mr. Tom Love	2.00
Dr. Maney	1.00
Mr. Julius Armour	1.00
Mrs. Evelyn Armour	1.00
Mr. J. B. Wright	2.00
Mr. R. J. Ruddy	2.50
Mr. Willie Ector	2.00
Mr. Napolean Frierson Sr.	1.00
Wonder Bread Co.	5.00
Mr. Freeland Reaves	2.00
Sallie Archable	3.00
Hazle Bowles	3.00
Hub City Bottling Works	5.00
Miss Helen B. Miller	1.00
Miss Cottrell Collier	1.00
Mrs. Arbure Clemmons	5.00
Mr. Diamond Beard	2.00
John Thomas Beard	1.00
Mr. C. W. Seay	1.00
Mrs. Lula May Lawrence	5.00
Mr. Marvin Creekware	4.00
Bessie Lou Shepherd	1.00
Mrs. Inez Jones	1.00
Mrs. A. K. Stiphens	1.00
Dr. M. Lay	5.00
Mr. J. C. Reaves	2.00
Mrs. Leslie Hamilton	2.00
Miss Garthelia Cavitt	4.50
Mr. Frank Blalock	10.00
Miss Emma Person	10.00
Mr. and Mrs. Jesse Bowles	5.00
Roberta Bass	1.00
Mr. E. R. Shockley	5.00
Mrs. Mariah McNeal	3.00
Mrs. Daisy Walton	3.00
Frierson Realty Co.	5.00
Mr. P. H. Exom	3.00
Dr. D. B. Grandberry	5.00
Mr. and Mrs. Gillis Johnson	2.00
Baker Mfg. Co.	10.00
Sommons Hdwe Co.	4.00
Mr. J. E. Hollingsworth	1.00
Mr. Joe Harris	1.00
Mrs. Effie Murphy	3.00
Mrs. J. W. Ashcraft	1.00
Mr. Austin Fentress	5.00
Mr. S. R. White	1.00
Mrs. Georgia Thates	1.00
Mrs. N. Dobbins	1.00
Mrs. Ethel Wilks	2.00
Mr. Raymon Wilks Sr.	3.00
Mr. Frank Norment	1.00
Dr and Mrs. Brooks	1.00
Mrs. Tissha May Tatum	1.00
Mr. Ollie Bufford	1.00
Mr. V. L. Robertson	5.00
Mrs. Marie Pitts	3.00
Mr. Dave Archable	5.00
Mrs. Lillian Harrison	1.00
Mrs. Helen Baley Jack	1.00
Mrs. Lula Newble	1.00
Vivian Clemmons	5.00
Bubbington Tlg. Co.	1.00

Gorup 3 — H. G. Norment
Robert Motley

H. G. Norment	5.00
Robert Motley	5.00
Zachariah Norment	2.00
Ben Murphy	5.00
Henry Neely	1.00

Frank Beard	2.00
Joel Bass	2.60
David Jackson	5.00
William Golden	1.00
Allen Shears	5.00
Jim Norment	3.00
Sam Notes	1.00
Jesse Bufford	2.00
Fred Murphy	3.00
Lemonia Allen	.50
Clover Garden CME Church	
	5.05
Antioch MB Church	5.10
Della Whitford	$10.00
Rev. E. D. Crisp	1.00
Mrs. Mary E. Crisp	1.00
Annie Notes	3.00
Mary E. Norment	2.00
Hattie Garner	3.00
Willie Rodgers	3.00
Elmer Murphy	3.00
Lucy Rhodes	1.00
Robert Spencer	1.00
Lawrence Reynolds	1.00
J. C. Reaves	2.00
Edye Ray Newborn	1.00
Mr. Summers	5.00
A. L. Smith	1.00
A. D. Powell	1.00
Gladys Wiley	1.00
Annie D. Bass	1.00
Lizzie M. McGuire	1.00
Johnie Ganett	2.00
Bernice Dawkins	2.05
Theodore Woods	1.00
Amanda McNeal	1.00
Agatha Lake	1.00
Elizabeth Ray	2.00
Lois Harris	1.00
Willie L. Bolden	1.00
Jim Bolden	1.50
Albert McNeal	1.00
Otha Motley	1.00
Prof. H. W. Harrison	1.00
Surleaster Crowder	3.15
Ora D. Norment	3.15
Ethel Ray Pirtle	3.15
Geneva Beard	3.15
Elise Mason	3.00
Lois Fleet	3.15
Edith Shockley	3.00
Mary Osler	3.00
Cora B. Puckett	3.00
Otherine Smith	3.10
Marie Bass	1.00
Ethe Lewis	3.00
Emanuel Parran	1.00
Clinton Wilkes	1.00
Bill Sweet	1.00
Louise Bufford	2.00
Leora Guy	2.25
Roxy Johnson	1.00
Nannie M. Morgan	1.00
Myrtle Newble	1.00
Robert Mewson	1.00
Ben Davis Polk	1.00
Rudolph L. White	1.00
Willie Ola Mewson	.75
Georgie Ola Rhodes	1.10
Dorothy Walton	1.00
Thomas Peay	1.00
Norlean Chambers	.50
Margrett McKinney	.50
Dornell Murphy	1.00

Group 4 — M. L. Robertson
Mr. Huley Shaw

M. L. Robertson	5.00
Huley Shaw	5.00
Mr. James Herron	5.00
Mr. Andrew Chambers	3.00
Mr. Robert Lambert Sr.	3.00
Whiteville Savings Bank	5.00
Mr. Charlie Lewis	2.50
Mr. Charle Mitchell	2.00
Mr. Ten Crowder	2.00
Mr. Horton Mosby	1.00
Fayette Parks	1.00
Mr. Jim Blakemore	1.00
Oak Grove Service Station,	
Mr. Frank Norment	1.00
Mr. Sam Pierce	1.00
Mr. Wash Browne	1.00
Mrs. Fannie Bell Shaw	3.00
Mrs. Rachel Shears	3.00
Mrs. Roberta Bass	3.00
Mrs. Nishie Pirtle	3.00
Mrs. Ida Norment	1.50
Pennie Goodman	1.50
Mrs. Ella Davis	1.00
Mrs. Mattie Price	1.00
Mrs. Lina Crowder	1.00
Lizzie Mae Franklin	1.00
Mae Ida McKinnie	4.50
Sammie Locket	3.50
Warlean Allen	3.15
Bessie Mae Parks	3.15
Susie Garner	3.00
Olivia Dodson	2.40
Joyce Marie Jones	2.25
Claude Perry	1.70
Lawrence McKinnie Jr.	1.50
Helen Miller	1.10
Virginia Miller	1.10
Ruby Ray Rodgers	1.00
William Ray Rhodes	1.00
Carnell Rhodes	1.00
Eugene Davis	1.00

Group 5 — W. R. Woods
Johnson Mays

Norman Rhodes	2.25
Hayes Reynolds	3.00
Johnson Mays	5.00
Charlie Rodgers	5.00
Gather Taylor	5.00
James Jones	1.00
Fannie Beard	1.00
Willie P. Jones	1.00
Hattie Woods	3.00
Lois Harris	2.50
Ada Curry	3.00
Bettye Randolph	1.00
J. D. Brown	1.00
E. B. Hudgens	1.00
Kora Patton	3.45
Sidney Taylor	1.00
W. R. Woods	5.00

Group 6 — D. R. Reed
Dr. G. A. Shelton

Mr. and Mrs. C. D. Haley	5.00
Mr. Frank Norment	1.00
Mr. Willie Davis	1.00
Mr. Lewis Morrow	5.00
Dr. G. A. Shelton	5.00
Mrs. S. N. Jones	3.50
Mrs. Lizzie Cross	4.50
Mrs. Susie Golden	1.25

Allen-White Basketball Pioneers
1934-1938
National and State Championship Teams

GIRLS	BOYS 1937-38	BOYS '47
Georgia L. Jenkins, Coach	J. H. White, Coach	George Meakins, Coac
	A.D. Hardy, Coach	
Bobbie Lou Lambert	Isaiah Harris	John T. Brady Jr.
Hattie Gardner	George Lewis	Thomas Finley
Mayme Lake	Mozell Lambert	Willie Golden
Julia Mae Wiley	John Ray	Tommy R. Sains
Ethel Tall	Frank Motley	James Scott
Rebecca Tall	Jimmie Cross	Usley Woods
Rubye Stallings	Walter Lewis	Edward Worthy
Dorothy Sparks		
Opal Motley		
Arlene Love		

BOYS	BOYS '41	GIRLS 1938-41
J. H. White, Coach	F. D. Fant, Coach	F. D. Fant, Coach
Maryland Flash Parker	Daniel Clark	Helen Shepherd
Floyd Coleman	Arthur Harris	Ethel Tyler
Robert (Jack) Green	Ellison Hudson	Martha Woods
Gernie Price	Neely Lake	Lydia Cheshier
Willie Walker	Robert Spencer	Zenobia Hamer
	James Teddy Jones	Beatrice Woods
		Helen Brown
		Annie Lockett
		Emma D. Herron
		Addie Woods
		Emma L. Tynes
		Marie Brady

Remarks by Evelyn C. Robertson Jr.
National Civil Rights Museum – Memphis, Tennessee
January 05, 2007

<u>Rosenwald Revisited</u>

Good Evening!

Let me thank those responsible for the Rosenwald Revisited, "Wisdom from Our Elders" project. I particularly would like to thank Ann Smithwick for her vision and her compassion for this project. I want to thank the Civil Rights Museum for its interest in hosting and organizing this event. I want to also thank the sponsors, especially Ford Motor Company. This effort has proven to be a real partnership.

This is a marvelous opportunity to rekindle interest and create awareness of education efforts for African Americans throughout the South at the turn of the twentieth century.

When Abraham Lincoln issued the Emancipation Proclamation in 1865, there were no publicly supported schools for African-Americans in the South. During the 1960s and 1970s many African-American communities in the south had their own schools which were publicly supported but had been built with a combination of private and public funds. After decades of integration, there is minimal presence of the existence of these schools that played such a tremendous role in bridging the chasm between the haves and the have nots. These schools are historic in every sense, and their contributions to society and the role that they played in the promotion of full citizenship to the downtrodden is immeasurable.

With the advent of integration and the elapse of time, it is a rarity to see a Rosenwald School. Where possible preservation of these schools should be a priority. Their legacy and the quest for full citizenship for African-American boys and girls with the preponderance of odds against them should be well documented. The abuses of slavery, Jim Crowism, persecution, inequality, discrimination and dehumanization should never be repeated against any race. The Rosenwald Schools played a significant role in mitigating these abuses and should be well documented and as a part of this nations heritage.

Allen-White High School in Whiteville, Tennessee was a Rosenwald school. A remnant of the physical plant exists today. There is strong interest and optimism in its restoration. The site is currently on the register as a state and national historic landmark, as determined by the U.S. Department of the Interior.

—The Allen-White School was Tennessee's first constructed all-brick Rosenwald school. It produced thirty-seven high school graduating classes, from 1933 – 1970. I am a proud graduate of the class of 1959. These graduates represented students and households from Hardeman County as well as eleven other Tennessee counties and Arkansas and Mississippi.

Allen-White graduates went on in life, entering colleges and universities across the nation and becoming part of the great migration of blacks from the South to the North, forming and participating in the urban communities and reinforcing the national workforce. In a great number of major urban cities throughout the South, people in leadership roles are Allen-White graduates or their descendents. The list of professionals that got their start at Allen-White covers the gamut, from farmers to educators to medical professionals, and includes at least one federal judge, in the person of the late Judge Odell Horton.—

For me, Allen-White School represented the cradle of knowledge, where young boys and girls could be inspired, nurtured, and equipped to venture onto life's journey. It was a place that you could dream dreams, even against tremendous societal odds.

For the past twenty years, every two years the alumni of Allen-White School has held an all school reunion. This past September represented one of the largest turnouts for this event in its history. We are continuing to thrive on the "Wisdom from the Elders."

Thanks very much for this opportunity and much success for the duration of the exhibit.

Remarks by Evelyn C. Robertson Jr.
A Victory Celebration Recognizing the 1940/1941
Allen-White Girl's National Champions

Antioch Baptist Church
November 23, 2008

To Pastor Boyle, Esteemed Allen-White champions, and audience all.

I am a proud 1959 graduate of Allen-White High School.

As I think of the history of Allen-White School, I think of it as a means of promoting the creed of Booker T. Washington of promoting self determination. He was one to promote picking themselves up by their bootstrap.

Allen-White's history dates to challenging times in our nation's history and to turbulent conditions in the South.

The history of this school existed in an era of so called "separate but equal," [and] even though the law sanctioned this concept, we know that there was no such thing as separate but equal during this era.

Despite all of that, there was determination, desire, sacrifice, [and] commitment, and there were extraordinary, visionary leaders that knew that there had to be a better day.

Allen-White School was more than about athletic prowess, it was about preparation for life. If you have the opportunity to read the bios of these surviving members of the 1940/41 championship team you can see that they were trailblazers in their own right and went on to successful careers in their chosen fields of endeavor.

I am in the process of some research about Allen-White for a forthcoming book describing the Allen-White story, its successes, and its ability to overcome obstacles and to preserver.

Fortunately, in my family there are collections of rarely seen photos, pamphlets, newspaper articles, programs from various events dating back to the '20s and '30s. This is compelling and inspiring and this story needs to be told.

I am glad to see the large numbers of young people here today. I wonder how many of you would be willing to ride a flat bed truck sixty miles a day from Grand Junction to Whiteville each day to get an education or to walk four to five miles each day through the rain and mud. Some had to board with residents who lived near the school because there was no bus route and walking was out of the question. This is the story of your great grandparents and in some instances your great great grandparents. It's their shoulders that you now stand on; to not give your best in your quest for an education is disrespect for their efforts and their sacrifices.

Tremendous interest has recently been shown about Allen-White over the past two years. As a Rosenwald school, its memorabilia and artifacts were on display at the National Civil Rights Museum in Memphis in 2006 and at the Little Courthouse Museum in Bolivar in 2008. I hope, ultimately, we will have a museum of our own to display these items permanently.

Interest in Rosenwald schools has peaked the interests of many citizens recently. Two weeks ago, the Fox News affiliate in Memphis did a two-part story of Woodstock High School in Shelby County, it was located in Lucy, Tennessee near Millington. It preceded Allen-White as a High School, my father was a graduate of Woodstock because at the time Allen-White did not exist.

Allen-White School traces its history to 1905.

Through the efforts of Mr. Jesse Christopher Allen, education in Whiteville progressed to the ultimate development of high school training for African American boys and girls.

The forerunner to Allen-White was the Hardeman County Training School, later named Allen-White High School.

It was James Herbert White of Gallatin, Tennessee that was the maker of the dream of Mr. Allen.

Some may not be aware, but between Mr. Allen and Mr. White there were two other principals, L. L. Campbell and G. W. Thomas of Chattanooga. After Mr. White's hiring and many successes it was later renamed Allen-White High School.

Between 1937 and 1942, Allen-White served as a boarding school. There were boys and girl's dormitories, serving students from twelve

Tennessee counties exclusive of Hardeman and from Mississippi and Arkansas.

Allen-White was highly successful in training boys and girls for their roles in adult life. The programs aroused interest of some of the educational leaders of Tennessee. Fisk University established an internship program.

Allen-White produced its first graduating class in 1933. Of the thirteen graduates, ten enrolled in college.

Following Dr. White's departure in 1948, Mr. Carl Seets became principal. Seets served as principal until 1952 when he was succeeded by Major A. Jarrett.

Allen-White served as the only high school for blacks in Hardeman County until 1960.

From 1933 until 1970, Allen-White sent graduates all over the U.S. and abroad. These graduates can be found in all walks of life, able to compete, and making worthwhile contributions in this modern, global society.

The legacy of Allen-White is forever etched into the fabric of our being and hopefully we will continue to keep its memory alive. This event this evening is a great expression of love and reverence for the accomplishments of this basketball team. Thank you for your attendance.

BIBLIOGRAPHY

Berneece, "What Allen-White has meant to me", *Allen-White Mirror Newspaper*, June 1937.

J.H. White, " Donors to Cheek Hal", *Allen-White Voice Newspaper*, December 19, 1941.

Author, "Allen-White High School." *Education Today and Tomorrow Journal*, (1948).

Author?. *A Chronicle of Black History in Hardeman County.* Bolivar, TN: Hardeman County Black History Committee, 1989.

Hancett, Tom, "Beacons for Black Education in the American South." Rosenwald Schools, "http://www.rosenwaldplans.org (posted 02/24/2006).

Hancett, Tom, "Saving the South's Rosenwald Schools." Rosenwald Schools, http://www.rosenwaldplans.org/history.html (posted 02/24/2006).

Maxwell, G. L. "Educating Youth for Citizenship." *Opportunity Journal of Negro Life* 19:1 (1941).

Hardeman County Tennessee 2007-2008 Community Guide. Bolivar, TN: Bolivar Bulletin-Times, Month Day?, 2007.

Rivers, Earnest et al. "In Memory of Jesse C. Allen, Founder of Allen-White School." *Bolivar Bulletin-Times*, Month Day, 1976.

Ross, Mecoy and Quinnie Armour. "The First Schools of Hardeman County." *Bolivar Bulletin-Times*, July 1976.

White, J. H., *The History of Allen-White School, 1905-1936,*

Woodard, C. Vann. *The Strange Career of Jim Crow,* 2nd ed. New York: Oxford Press, 1966.

Woods, Jerry, W. "The Julius Rosenwald Fund School Building Program: A Saga in the Growth and Development of African-American Education in Selected West Tennessee Communities." EdD diss., University of Mississippi, 1995.

Additional Reading

Ascoli, Peter Max, "Julius Rosenwald: The Man Who Built Sears, Roebuck and Advanced the Cause of Black Education in the American South", Indiana University Press, 2006

Harlan, Louis, Booker T. Washington: "The Wizard of Tuskegee, 1901-1915", New York: Oxford University Press, 1983.

Hoffschwelle, Mary S, "The Rosenwald Schools of the American South", University of Florida Press, 2006.

Rivers, Earnest, L. "The History of Allen-White High School, Whiteville Hardeman County, TN from 1930-1948," Masters thesis, Tennessee State A&I, 1954.

White, J. H., "Up From a Cotton Patch", J. H. White and the development of Mississippi Valley State College, Itta Bena, MS: Mississippi Valley State College Press, 1979.

ABOUT THE AUTHOR

I was born November 19, 1941 in Winchester, Tennessee to Evelyn Sr. and Pearl Robertson. The oldest of three boys, I entered Allen-White School in 1946.

At fourteen, and just prior to entering the ninth grade, tragedy struck my family. My father was the victim of a homicide in July of 1955, and my mother was left to raise three boys, fourteen, twelve, and six, by herself. As fate would have it, and through God's Providence, my aunt, Myrtle L. Robertson, my father's sister, stepped boldly up to the plate and played an indelible role in supporting my mother in raising my brothers, Darnell and James, and me. I owe the molding, the love, the compassion, the nurturing, and the character building I experienced to these two ladies. Without their love, support, and devotion I could never have become the person that I am.

I am also grateful for the "village" that provided me support and nurturing. I know that it does take a village to raise a child. Just a few of the village characters that were present and important in my upbringing were: Rev. L. Nelson, pastor of the Elcanaan Baptist Church; Earnest Rivers, teacher and coach; Jesse I. Norment, teacher, coach, and scoutmaster; Charlie Nelson Stallings, assistant scoutmaster; Robert Motley; Elma Motley; W. D. Greene; Blanche Greene; Johnny G. Curtis; George Curtis; Norman Rhodes; Mabel Rhodes; Walker White; Susie White;

Hulie Shaw; Fannie B. Shaw; H. G. Norment; Lillie B. Rivers; Minerva Jarrett; Bernice Dawkins Stallings; Zeb Cross; Ada Curry; Jimmy Cross; Margaret Sanders and Alexander Sanders.

In 1959, at seventeen, I entered Tennessee State University as a freshman, and earned a Bachelor of Science Degree in Political Science and History in 1962, at age twenty. In August of 1962, I joined the faculty of the Allen-White High School, my alma mater. In 1963, I married Hugholene Ellison, who was teaching in the Hardeman County School System at the time. We raised two children, Jeffrey and Sheila, who currently are both successful in their respective careers.

In 1969, I received a Master's Degree from Tennessee State University with a major in Administration and Supervision. I did further study at Memphis State University, now the University of Memphis. During my tenure at Allen-White, I taught Social Studies, World History, Drivers Education, and coached boys basketball. On the faculty at Allen-White during my tenure, was my Aunt Myrtle, who taught Home Economics for forty years.

During the school year 1969-70, I was appointed principal at the Allen-White Elementary School, grades K-6. With the advent of full desegregation in 1970, I was appointed vice principal at Central High School in Bolivar, TN. I served in this capacity until May of 1974.

In June of 1974, I accepted a position as assistant superintendent of community services at Western Mental Health Institute in Bolivar, TN. I served in this capacity for five years. In 1979, I was appointed by the Commissioner of the Department of Mental Health and Mental Retardation as the founding Superintendent of the Nat T. Winston Developmental Center. This inpatient facility served dually diagnosed adults (mental illness secondary to mental retardation). At the time of its establishment, it was the only facility of its type in the nation. The facility was fully accredited in two years.

In 1983, I accepted the appointment to the superintendency of Western Mental Health Institute, a psychiatric facility in Bolivar, TN. This facility provided inpatient psychiatric services to citizens in twenty-one counties of western Tennessee. I served in this capacity until January 1991. In 1991, the then governor of the state of Tennessee, Ned Ray

McWherter, asked me to join his cabinet as the commissioner of the Tennessee Department of Mental Health and Mental Retardation. I accepted this offer and served four years in this role. The department had a budget exceeding $350 million and thousands of employees. The cornerstone of my tenure as commissioner was the development of a master plan for the delivery of comprehensive mental health services throughout the state of Tennessee. Components of that plan are still being implemented. I also had the honor of serving as president of the National Association of State Mental Health Program Directors (NASMHPD) in 1994. This organization represented mental health commissioners throughout the country, including Guam. My tenure as commissioner ended in January of 1995. I then joined West Tennessee Health Care in Jackson, Tennessee for approximately a year and a half as vice president of behavioral health. Following my brief tenure at West Tennessee Health Care, I was appointed executive director of the Southwest Tennessee Development District in Jackson, TN. I served in this capacity for eleven years, retiring in August of 2007. I also served as a county commissioner, serving on the Hardeman County Commission for thirteen years. During that tenure, I never had an opponent. My forty-five plus years of professional life afforded me many opportunities, as well as challenges. I attribute any successes I had to the foundation that I received while at Allen-White School.

Growing up in the segregated South, where blacks were considered inferior, it never dawned on me that there were boundaries or limitations as to what I might achieve or attain in life. I knew from an early age that education was the key to attaining success in life. This was emphasized in my home, as my father and two aunts were college graduates. Many of the people that I was surrounded by in the church and in the community were college graduates and served as role models. My grandfather, even though not educated, was instrumental in the establishment of the Allen-White School, serving as treasurer of the board of trustees. He obviously understood how valuable education could be.

The separate water fountains, the separate lunch counters, the separate schools, having to use side entrances to theaters, using back doors to white residences—as deplorable and denigrating as these practices were—did not marginalize my desire to be the best that I could be. With my family's support and encouragement, and my faith in God, I knew that there had to be better days ahead.

In 1959, when I entered Tennessee State University (TSU), it was the beginning of a very turbulent period in the history of this country. With advent of the Civil Rights Movement, the desegregation of lunch counters, intrastate travel, and other public accommodations, such as access to theaters, parks, hotels, and museums, college students throughout the South were instrumental in breaking down these barriers through peaceful protests that included marches, sit-ins, and arrests. As a student at TSU, I had not only the opportunity to see this process unfold, but to participate in it. My first two years of college were filled with attendance at mass meetings, marches, and sit-ins. The efforts of the students at Tennessee State University, Fisk, and Meharry, as well as other institutions, played a very important role in striking down the barriers that had inhibited black progress and inclusion throughout the South and other parts of the country. The efforts did not come without a price. Some students were spit on, pushed, shoved, jailed, and some were expelled from school. Even peaceful resistance was not an acceptable course of action by the authorities in 1960 and 1961. The experience of this movement and the continued belief by the majority race that blacks were neither entitled nor deserved respect and equality, emboldened my desire to achieve all that was within my grasp.

Upon my return to Hardeman County in August of 1962, as a part of my interview for a teaching position, I was asked by the then superintendent of schools, Mr. Ben Carr, what role I played in the "confusion," as he put it, in Nashville.

My college experience played a very important role in shaping my persona. As I embarked on my professional career, I embraced the qualities of intelligence, respect, tolerance, patience, and humility. I expect the same from my fellow man. These qualities have served me well in my many endeavors, and continue to serve me today. My personal Mission Statement is : To serve God, Family and Fellowman in a manner that embraces the golden rule.

Made in the USA
Lexington, KY
03 September 2018